THE HANDBOOK OF SOUTHERN VEGETABLE GARDENING

D1558899

Barbara Pleasant

Peachtree Publishers, Limited

Published by
PEACHTREE PUBLISHERS, LTD.
494 Armour Circle, N.E., Atlanta, Georgia 30324

Copyright © 1984 Barbara Pleasant

Design by Cynthia McDaniel
Jacket Photograph by Joe McTyre
Illustrations by Walter Cumming

Manufactured in the United States

First Edition

Library of Congress Catalog Number 83-63499

ISBN: 0-931948-56-8

To my gardening partner.

TABLE OF CONTENTS

FOREWORD

It doesn't take much to convince Southerners to plant gardens. Give them a shovel, a handful of seeds, and a spot in the sunshine, and they'll surely try to grow something — and probably succeed. We live in a climate that brings out the gardener in all of us, even if it means being tortured by mosquitoes or harassed by weeds. Why do we do it? There are plenty of reasons.

Perhaps the most compelling reason to garden is the feeling of panic we get in the produce section at the supermarket. Flabbergasted by the high cost and low quality of the vegetables there, we say, "What? Five dollars for a bag of potatoes? Eighty cents a pound for pithy tomatoes?" Then we go home, kick ourselves for awhile, and resolve to do something about it. We plant gardens.

Not just ordinary gardens, either. We plant *Southern gardens,* which are remarkably different from those in other parts of the country. The traditional Southern vegetable garden includes crops which the native Indians shared with our ancestors, (squash, corn, and beans) some others brought by the Africans (watermelons, field peas, and okra), and, of course, a few foods favored by our European forebears (cabbage, onions, and herbs). But the modern South, like other cultures, has become more cosmopolitan, and nowadays we want to grow many new vegetables — food plants our fathers and grandfathers never tried, or tried and failed with — such as broccoli, spinach, and oriental vegetables. These are the vegetables we pay so dearly for, since they have to be shipped to us from thousands of miles away. But, as any experienced gardener will tell you, simply *wanting* to grow a certain vegetable won't make it happen. First you have to learn how.

Here in the South, the cultural instructions for growing many vegetables are very different from the way you'd go about it if you lived in New England or somewhere in the Rocky Mountains. Perhaps the biggest difference is the warm weather

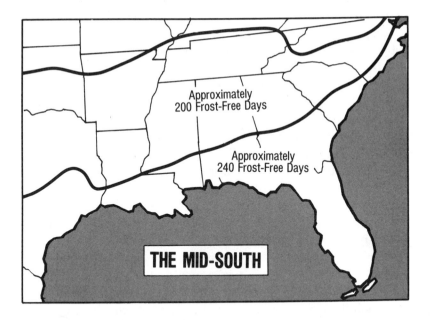

Approximately 200 Frost-Free Days

Approximately 240 Frost-Free Days

THE MID-SOUTH

orientation of our whole ecology. Warmth is dominant. Cool is transitional. Cold is short-lived. What this means to the gardener is that growing food is not just a summertime thing. Frequently we need to plant at strange times of the year. Vegetables which need cool weather or those which bugs love to munch must be grown in spring and fall, when insect populations are low. To avoid a heat stroke in the summer sun, we must arrange our crop so that we have little gardening work to do in midsummer. Our long growing season sets the stage for a distinctive type of gardening, which is unlike gardening in any other part of the world. Southern gardening.

The truth is that it doesn't take much effort to grow food in our climate, as long as you pay attention to what you're doing. The information in this book will help you to understand the major trends and minor intricacies in your garden — a handbook to refer to as you learn how the Southern vegetable garden works.

I've written with an emphasis on organic gardening, which is different from and yet much the same as any other type of gardening. The only point I really want to stress is that organic gardening *does* work in the South. Garden insects really *can* be managed without using synthetic pesticides, which is the main objection I hear to caring for a Southern garden organically. Certainly there may be pest-related failures once in a while, which the timely application of some chemical may have prevented, but not very often. Most of the time the use of the right organic method can solve any gardening problem that develops.

Besides, some of the personal reasons why people garden in the first place don't jibe with the use of chemicals, which may cause unexpected harm to your soil, your water supply, or even your health. Many people enjoy the sense of adventure that comes from getting involved with nature and watching plants and animals in the garden explode with life. They're fascinated by earthworms, honeybees, frogs, birds, and thousands of six-legged things. Other folks just like to get outside for some slow-paced exercise, and then have something delicious to show for their effort. Many families garden together; parents are anxious to teach their children about nature in a setting where they can see, touch, and taste the wonder of living things firsthand. None of these reasons — gardening for intellectual stimulation, for your health, or doing it to share with your kids — meshes with the indiscriminate use of toxic chemicals. You really can do without them.

But no matter how you garden, remember to have fun. Take it too seriously, and you'll start blaming yourself for things that happen because of the weather, poor seed quality, or any other of a number of gardening problems which really have little to do with you. For a hobby to be productive, you should enjoy doing it — not because you have to, but because you want to. Hopefully this handbook will help you to grow the wonderful garden you've been dreaming of this year. And next year. And for the rest of your gardening life.

1
SOIL CARE
AND FERTILIZATION

Everyone wants to know the secret of growing a successful garden, but there is no secret. The primary factor and ultimate determinant of the quality of a garden is the quality of the soil.

Yet even good soil can misbehave if the garden site is poorly drained or shaded for most of the day. Most vegetables grow best in full sun, though beans and some leafy vegetables perform well in partial shade. When choosing a home for your garden, pick a place where rainwater disappears within hours after a thunderstorm — standing water indicates chronic poor drainage. Such places are highly susceptible to soil diseases, and they stay muddy for a long time after every rain. An ideal garden site has a slight slope and a southern or western exposure. Trees along the northern rim of the garden can be beneficial as a windbreak, but other trees close to the garden tend to block out sun and clutter the garden soil with tough, unwanted roots. So make sure you've chosen the best site available before starting to work on improving your garden soil.

Good soil is something to be understood and admired. Some people think of soil as something dead, and they call it dirt. As gardeners, such people are forever amateurs, for really good soil is anything but dead. It's actually an active community of various forms of microscopic life, which share their home with the roots of growing plants. These micro-inhabitants eat *organic matter* in order to produce plant food.

Organic matter is anything that used to be living and now is dead and rotten, such as leaves, stems, and bark. Once they decompose, these materials become the soil constituents which provide food for growing plants. It is true that much of the mass, or content, of soil is nothing more than finely chopped rocks. But good garden soil, which often is described as loose, loamy, and friable, is much more than a jumble of crushed rocks. It also contains numerous particles of organic matter.

In addition to serving as plant food, organic matter improves the texture of the soil by increasing its ability to hold water and air. How this works depends on the consistency of the soil to start with. Is it sand or clay? Sandy soils have large soil particles, while clay is made up of tiny ones. In sand, the spaces between particles are large and coarse. In clay, these spaces are tight and constricted. When organic matter is added to sand, the spaces between the particles become partially blocked by the new materials, which increases the soil's ability to retain water. When water does flow through enriched sand, it becomes saturated with nutrients from the organic matter which subsequently are taken up by plants. When organic matter is added to clay, the tight spaces between soil particles are opened up, so that water can percolate better and air doesn't get squeezed out so easily. This is the physical side of soil health. If the soil is in good shape physically, plant roots can easily penetrate in search of food.

But what will roots find? Hopefully nitrogen, phosphorous, potassium, magnesium, aluminum, calcium, and as many as fifty other nutrients. If they don't find what they're looking for, the obvious solution is to place plant food in the soil. Chemical fertilizers, in either granular or liquid form, contain the basic nutrients needed by plants, and many people use them. However, most plants need much more than what chemical fertilizers have to offer. They cannot live on nitrogen, potassium, and phosphorous alone. Plants also require minerals, trace nutrients, and a soil environment that makes it easy for roots to forage for what they need.

Poor soil of any type can be turned easily into good soil. The key is rotten organic matter — leaves, manures, straw, grass clippings, sawdust, peanut hulls, etc. These substances break down into forms that plant roots can convert easily into food, and they also leave fibers behind in the soil which absorb water

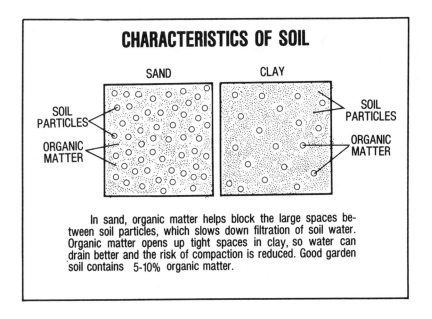

CHARACTERISTICS OF SOIL

SAND   CLAY

SOIL
PARTICLES

ORGANIC
MATTER

SOIL
PARTICLES

ORGANIC
MATTER

In sand, organic matter helps block the large spaces between soil particles, which slows down filtration of soil water. Organic matter opens up tight spaces in clay, so water can drain better and the risk of compaction is reduced. Good garden soil contains 5-10% organic matter.

and air, thus improving the soil's texture, or tilth. Soil which is rich in rotten organic matter is ideal for growing vegetables.

Rotten is a key word here. Unrotted organic matter is not ready for use by plants; in fact, the rotting process often temporarily ties up nutrients already present in the soil. To make the best use of organic soil amendments, set them aside to rot and then add them to the soil. When various substances are combined and allowed to rot together, the result is compost, nature's most perfect plant food.

THE CASE FOR COMPOSTING

Finished compost is health food for garden plants. It contains a broad array of nutrients and chemicals which plants need, but unlike "instant" chemical fertilizers, the nutrients in compost are released slowly to plants. Meanwhile, spongy bits of fiber leftover from the original ingredients absorb soil water, feed earthworms and other soil organisms, and help to keep the soil soft and airy.

Making compost is similar to cooking — you combine the ingredients, wait for them to "cook," and then feed the finished product to garden plants. Composts work faster in warm weather than in cold weather, since the soil organisms which cause the rotting process to occur are most active when temperatures are above fifty degrees. The time required for compost to mature also depends on the ingredients used. Manures rot very fast, while tough plant fibers, like okra stalks, take much longer. But once a compost heap becomes active, anything you add to it will rot quickly. I suggest that all gardeners keep at least one compost heap going at all times.

Here's how to get started:

STEP ONE: Delegate a six-foot square area for your compost heap, and locate it near a water faucet. Collect as many different kinds of organic matter as you can find, including but not limited to leaves; grass clippings; horse, goat, chicken, or cow manure; vegetable trimmings from the kitchen; chopped weeds; hay or straw.

STEP TWO: Place these ingredients in two-inch layers, adding a layer of plain garden soil every third layer. Water the heap as you build it. At this point, you can't add too much water. All ingredients must be moist or they will not rot.

STEP THREE: Build the heap until it is at least two and a half feet tall, preferably taller. Cover the heap with leaves, straw, or plastic to keep it from drying out. Let it sit for two to three weeks. Meanwhile, continue to collect more ingredients to add later.

STEP FOUR: After three weeks, chop the heap apart (a mattock is the perfect tool for this). As you chop, add any new ingredients you have obtained, and water to help correct moisture imbalances. Pile everything into a heap again, and let it sit for another three weeks.

STEP FIVE: At this point, the compost should be very active. It will steadily shrink in size. Continue to chop it up every few weeks — this incorporates air into the heap, which bacteria need to do their best work. As the bacteria work, the temperature of the heap should rise, in some cases as high as one hundred and twenty degrees. However, composts which contain

4

more than twenty parts carbon (leaves and other tree parts are mostly carbon) to one part nitrogen (manures from grain-fed animals are mostly nitrogen) may not heat up as they decompose. To increase the nitrogen content of the heap, add cottonseed meal, blood meal, or alfalfa meal as you chop. Once the heap is active, you can add much of your kitchen refuse to the heap by removing a couple of shovelfuls from the center of the heap, dropping the new ingredients in, and covering it up again.

STEP SIX: Finished compost is dark colored and crumbly. Use it freely with your vegetable plants, but also set some aside to help activate your next heap. Since finished compost contains large numbers of the microorganisms which speed up rotting, new heaps start working faster if mature compost is layered in along with the raw ingredients.

The greatest demand for compost will come in spring and late summer, when most vegetables are planted. Start your spring compost heap in the fall when leaves are plentiful, and set up another heap in early summer when grass clippings are easy to find. If you think the composting process sounds like a lot of boring work, you're wrong. It's actually a fascinating process to watch, and the finished product is the best insurance possible when it comes to seeing that your vegetable plants are adequately fed. Compost is a valuable addition to potting soils for houseplants, too.

SHEET COMPOSTING, GREEN MANURES, AND MULCHES

Besides composting in piles, there are other ways to enrich garden soil. Manures can be added to the soil directly, or they can be spread over the soil surface and covered with a mulch. This is called *sheet composting*, since the compostable materials are spread over the garden in sheets. Sheet composting works very well when it's done in the fall. The materials break down during the winter months and may be turned under in spring.

When sheet composting with animal manures, don't use manures from animals that graze in permanent pastures. Horses and cows eat numerous weed seeds, which have no trouble sprouting after they've passed through the animals' systems. Compost weed-bearing manure in hot compost (this kills many weed seeds), or set it aside and use it to make "manure tea" — a wonderful liquid fertilizer. Chicken manure and manures from grain-fed animals contain few weed seeds and are best to use for sheet composting.

Green manures are another way to increase the organic content of garden soil, but actually they are not manures at all. Green manures are living plant matter that's turned under to rot. Clovers, grains, immature weeds, and any other plants that are chopped into the soil while lush and green are green manures. As the leaves and roots rot, they add to the humus content of the soil.

Green manuring works best in large gardens where space is cheap. Green manure, or "cover" crops, also help choke out weeds, so it's an ideal treatment for new areas being used for growing vegetables for the first time. Buckwheat is a fast-growing cover crop for warm weather, but most people prefer to grow green manures in fall and winter, when only a few vegetables can be grown. Winter wheat and oats are hard to beat as winter cover crops. Plant them in fall, mow the topgrowth down in the middle of winter, and turn them under as soon as the soil dries in spring. Clovers make good green manures, too, but they don't give the kind of short-term return you'll get with buckwheat and winter grains.

Mulches are perhaps the greatest innovation of the century in vegetable gardening, but the idea of using mulches to control weeds is far from new. The Mayan Indians of Central America used mulches thousands of years ago, and their agricultural success helped them to build an empire. Modern research has shown that a good mulch can increase vegetable production substantially while cutting down on other gardening chores, particularly watering and weeding. It's also a great thing to do for your soil.

What is a mulch? Any organic material that is spread over the garden's surface in a thick layer, thus forming a permeable barrier between the soil and the air, qualifies as a mulch. The

6

most common materials used in Southern gardens are leaves, grass clippings, hay, and shredded bark. Mulches help feed garden soil as they slowly rot, eventually becoming humus. Vegetables grown surrounded by mulch benefit greatly, since mulches filter and hold water for plant roots and help moderate the temperature of the soil. As rain trickles through a mulch, the drops absorb water-soluble nutrients, which in turn help feed plant roots. Mulches also block out the sunlight which weed seeds need to germinate.

Just about any dead plant material can be used as a mulch. Hay and leaves are easy to find and easy to use, though the list of possible mulch materials is much longer than this. Recent research findings suggest that peanut hulls may double yields of corn and beans; if you can find them, you've hit the jackpot. When you need a mulch in a hurry, simply lay down sections of newspaper, six to eight sheets thick, and cover with shredded bark, soil, or anything else to keep them from blowing away. All mulches prevent soil erosion. Under a protective cover of mulch, the organic matter you've added to your soil won't be washed away by the first rainstorm that comes along.

MINERAL AND ROCK FERTILIZERS
Last but not least, ground rock fertilizers and other mineral fertilizers go a long way in boosting soil fertility. Minerals such as lime and rock phosphate help to "unlock" other soil nutrients and facilitate the nutrient uptake of plants. These substances may be incorporated directly into the soil, added to compost, or mixed with water to form a "slurry" used as a booster feeding for growing plants.

LIME
Most Southern soils are acidic. While certain vegetables thrive in acidic soil, most of them prefer a pH that's only a little on the acid side. Ground limestone reduces soil acidity, and most Southern gardens need liming every two to three years. For best results, dust the garden surface with lime in early winter and either till it in or cover with a mulch to keep it from washing away. By spring, the lime will have worked its magic —

a process that takes several months. Lime can be applied at planting time, too, but since it's more of a soil conditioner than a fertilizer, it's best to apply it in the fall.

WOOD ASHES

Wood ashes are one of the most versatile and useful substances to keep on hand. They repel many insects when dusted over plants. When dug or watered into the soil, wood ashes supply large amounts of potassium, a basic plant nutrient. They also help mitigate extreme acidity in the soil. Arrange to collect ashes from friends who heat their homes with wood, and keep them dry until needed. Coal ashes are completely different from wood ashes and have little to offer the garden.

ROCK PHOSPHATE

This is a magical fertilizer. It supplies large amounts of phosphorous and also enhances nitrogen that's present in the soil from other sources. It's a strange marriage, but experiments consistently have shown that ground rock phosphate increases the amount of nitrogen made available to plants, especially when it's added to compost during the latter stages of decomposition. Additionally, this powder may be worked into the soil where it acts as a time-release fertilizer for three or more months. Many suppliers have dropped ground rock phosphate and sell superphosphate instead. This fertilizer is faster acting than rock phosphate but is not quite as good in terms of soil building.

GRANITE DUST

This is another mineral fertilizer that's widely available. Ground up granite rock supplies potash in much the same way that rock phosphate supplies phosphorous. It's best applied in the fall and stays in the soil for several months.

GREENSAND

Greensand is another good source of potash. It also contains numerous other trace elements that plants need for optimum growth. Greensand comes from undersea ocean deposits and tends to be rather expensive. However, it's an ideal fertilizer to keep on hand, especially if your compost supply is short. Think of it as a broad-spectrum fertilizer that helps balance the other organic amendments you add to the soil. Greensand often is hard to find and may have to be purchased by mail.

DRIED MEAL FERTILIZERS

Bone meal, blood meal, cottonseed meal, and other "flours" made from organic materials help fortify soil fertility. They contain much nitrogen as well as other plant nutrients. Since they can be quite costly, most gardeners use them for activating compost or for feeding pet plants. However, they also may be dug directly into the soil in small amounts. Water them in well before planting seeds or seedlings, for they release their nutrients quickly and can give small plants more nutrients than they can handle.

PUTTING IT ALL TOGETHER

There is no right and wrong way to keep soil fertile and healthy, but some ways are definitely better than others. Obviously plants remove nutrients from the soil, and it's up to the gardener to put those nutrients back. Reliance on chemical fertilizers ultimately shortchanges your soil and your plants, for these products supply only the major plant nutrients — not the long list of nutrients that plants need to flourish. Once the zinc, calcium, aluminum, boron, and other trace nutrients are gone, you can get them back only by adding *real* organic fertilizers to the soil. Worn-out soil that's enriched with "convenience" fertilizers remains relatively infertile. It may be okay for soybeans, but it's inadequate for lush, finicky vegetables.

It is certainly possible to use chemical fertilizers in conjunction with organic ones, but try to think of them only as a supplement. Just as people take vitamins to make sure that they get their minimum quota of nutrients, using chemical fertilizers as supplements for crops that are heavy feeders sometimes helps. However, if you use enough compost, manure, and other organic soil amendments, you will have no need for bagged chemical fertilizers, and your soil will be in much better condition. If you do use chemical fertilizers, look for ones that contain

9

trace nutrients as well as nitrogen, phosphorous, and potassium.

Once organic processes begin, and the soil becomes active with the forms of life that cause natural decomposition, the soil can, to some extent, renew itself. You just have to give it the right materials to work with.

2
PEACEFUL COEXISTENCE WITH WEEDS

The first big gardening problem of the season is weeds — those wild plants that appear like magic in any place where sunshine touches bare soil. The Southern eye of nature doesn't like her soil surface scarred and open, so she quickly covers the "wounds" with weed plants. And she's very good at it. Her planting agents include the wind, birds, and the bottoms of your shoes. As extra insurance, some weed seeds have thicker seed-coats than others — just the equipment needed to remain viable for years. Many weed plants can produce ten thousand seeds or more in a few weeks or even days. Gardeners take on quite a task when they pit themselves against such a powerful force.

But you *can* garden and, in the process, even get the weeds working on your side — you just have to organize them a little. Some weeds will appear in your garden no matter what you do, so you may as well accept them and put them to work. How? Cut them down and use them as mulch, or pull them up and add them to the compost heap, or prevent them from sprouting in the first place by covering the soil with a mulch. You can do many things with weeds, but you cannot allow them to grow freely alongside your vegetables. Weeds are experts at drawing nutrients from the soil, and they successfully beat out vegetables for food and space.

But controlling weeds is quite different from eradicating them altogether. Very few gardening situations require that every last weed be plucked out. Carrots, onions, and a few other vegetables do demand constant weeding, until the seedlings are big enough to claim their own space, but most vegetables can cope with *some* weed competition. A few weeds scattered here and there also can help you keep track of what's going on with garden insects. One of the few benefits that weeds offer is to help "balance" insect populations by increasing the diversification of plants in the garden.

Still, there are good weeds and there are bad weeds, and how to handle all garden weeds should be determined by what style of garden you have. Is it an intensive garden, a semi-intensive garden, or a large garden that includes many row crops?

In an *intensive* or raised bed garden, it's feasible to keep almost all weeds out, both because small-scale elimination of weeds is possible, and because you need every inch of space for growing vegetables. You can create your own diversified garden ecology by planting herbs and flowers among your vegetables and by juxtaposing different food plants. Weed control in an intensive garden is relatively simple, especially when mulches are used. The few weeds that do appear are easy to snatch out.

In a *semi-intensive* garden, where you have some raised beds, some row crops, and generally a lot going on, vigilance is required to keep weeds in their place. That place always should be subordinate to the vegetables being grown. In other words, weeds have gone too far when they're growing faster, taller, and in greater numbers than the vegetables. The best control measures are to cut weeds down with a sharp hoe, and never to allow any weeds to go to seed in the garden. Nonetheless, this type of garden can tolerate and even benefit from a few selected weeds. Red-rooted pigweed, for example, is good to have around since flea beetles, blister beetles, and several other destructive insects like it. If the pigweed is being eaten, you'll know the bugs are there, and you can take steps to protect other plants. Still, remove about ninety-five percent of the weeds that pop up — even the useful ones. Too many will serve as beacons to wandering bugs who may decide that dinner at your place is starting to look too good to pass up. Use mulches whenever possible to keep the number of all weeds at a minimum.

In a *large* garden which includes many row crops, it's important to weed early and regularly. Cultivate with your tiller when seedlings are small, making sure that the tines are set shallow. Cultivating deeper than three inches may injure plant roots as well as increase future weed problems by dragging buried weed seeds to the surface. Machine cultivation doesn't affect the weeds that come up in the row between vegetable plants; these must be pulled out by hand. If there are only a few of them, don't worry. They will help vary the plant population and may confuse some insects. Just don't let them take over, and see that the worst ones never get a foothold. Use cover crops to choke out weeds when large blocks of space will not be used for several months. Fall-planted oats, rye, or wheat are excellent cover crops for controlling weeds, and the tops can be cut in spring and used as mulch. Many keepers of large gardens shun mulches because they think they're too much work to collect and put down. But compared to hoeing for several hours every week, the time required to lay down a good mulch is time well spent.

SEPARATING THE GOOD WEEDS FROM THE BAD

You'll need to kill a few weeds, regardless of the type of garden you have. Which ones should you go after first? Generally, perennial and biennial weeds (not to be confused with annual weeds which reseed successfully year after year) are the most difficult ones to eliminate. There are hundreds of these which inhabit Southern gardens, including yuccas, Johnson grass, and bermuda grass. These and other long-lived weeds have death-defying roots, which make them a frustrating presence in the garden. Attempting to control them by tilling them away can increase the problem, too. It takes only a tiny section of viable root to grow into a thriving new weed plant. So don't try to till perennial weeds away; dig them out with a shovel. Bermuda grass and other tenacious perennial grasses respond well to the suffocating effects of a good mulch. For best results, leave the mulch in place for at least six months.

Weeds that grow as vines are another group of wild plants to keep out of the garden. Morning glories are perfect examples.

13

They look innocent as seedlings, but they grow fast and twist themselves around anything that sticks out of the ground. Control these and other vining weeds by hoeing them down when they're young, and by never allowing them to drop seeds in the garden.

There are good weeds, too, such as clover-type weeds, vetches, and other legumes. These weeds are able to change nitrogen from the air into a usable food. They store this nitrogen in their roots until flowering begins, at which time they use it up. If you hoe them down in mid-life, they can actually help build the nitrogen content of the soil. Even if allowed to flower, legumes leave cultures of nitrogen-fixing bacteria in the soil that later can go to work for beans and peas. Clovers and vetches help lure beneficial insects to the garden, too. Still, they do compete with vegetables for soil nutrients, and, as you might expect, too much of even a good weed is a bad thing.

There are many other weeds that can be helpful in the garden under the right circumstances. Some can even assist you when it comes to insect control. It's undeniable that weed season and bug season coincide, and one feeds off the other. It's all very complex, but some eating insects will forget about ravaging vegetables if they run across the right tasty weed. The only way to know which weeds are preferred by destructive insects is to pay close attention and learn from firsthand observations of your garden. The weed and insect life in your garden probably will not be the same as those in other people's gardens. Learning which weeds lure eating insects away from which vegetables may take a few seasons, but this knowledge will help to make your Southern garden healthier and stronger, and ultimately will cut down on the work you have to do to keep it in prime condition.

A FEW WEEDS WORTH KNOWING

Morning glory

Morning glories remove nitrogen and other important soil nutrients and produce many seeds. Beneficial only to bush beans, and then in small numbers. Mexican bean beetles feed on leaves.

Cocklebur

Indicates low soil fertility. Tough to get rid of if allowed to grow to maturity. No beneficial properties.

Pigweed

Also called lambs-quarters. Eaten by young striped cucumber beetles, blister beetles, and flea beetles. Remove most of them, for they feed heavily and each plant produces thousands of seeds.

Vetch

Fixes nitrogen. Remove before flowers appear to keep nitrogen in the soil.

3

CONTROLLING GARDEN PESTS

Insects and other pests are a naturally occurring phenomenon in all vegetable gardens. Insect populations tend to be quite high in the warm, damp climate of the South, yet many natural forces keep them in check — the weather; large predators, such as birds, bats, and frogs; fellow insect predators; and you, the gardener. The garden is a little ecosystem, and, as such, it polices itself and maintains a balance among its various inhabitants. However, growing big, beautiful vegetables often does not fit into nature's plan, and sooner or later you have to step in and take an active role in protecting your plants. After all, growing vegetables instead of weeds in the garden plot is your idea, so you can't expect nature to do all the work.

Prevention of insect problems is the logical first step in protecting your plants. Healthy, well-fed plants resist insect attack much better than struggling ones, and you'll have fewer insect problems if your soil is in good condition. Additionally, various soil diseases which are passed on by insects will have a hard time getting established in soil that is well cared for. Other methods of protecting plants from pests include interplanting, practicing good garden sanitation, and rotating crops from year to year. These are the major ways to reduce the probability that pests will seriously damage garden plants.

INTERPLANTING
Mixing up plantings a bit, so that large groups of the same vegetable do not stand together, is called interplanting. Different vegetables may be grown side by side, or herbs and flowers can be added to vegetable plots. Interplanting encourages the attention of hundreds of different kinds of insects, which in turn

17

increases the probability that the *harmful* insects will be bothered by insect predators. It's a very good sign to see different species of insects flitting here and there in the garden, especially during the morning hours when summer insects are most active.

This balance between good insects and bad insects is an important characteristic of the Southern environment that gardeners need to understand. Since we humans live in bug-free indoor environments, it's easy for us to conceive of insects in general as a hostile force. But actually bees, wasps, and flies are among the most helpful of garden insects. Large, fierce-looking beetles are beneficial, too — they feed on other insect larvae in the soil. Little red beetles with black spots (or white ones with black spots) are lady beetles, which feed on aphids and other small insects. A healthy population of lady beetles will take care of most of the tiny bugs which bother garden plants.

KEEP THE GARDEN CLEAN

Very mobile insects seldom stay in one place long enough to do much damage. On the other hand, most harmful insects are limited in their mobility — they hatch, feed, and reproduce without moving far from their favorite host plants. Because of this, a thorough fall cleanup of garden debris goes a long way toward reducing the numbers of destructive insects — the ones that make it through the winter and wait patiently in soil and dead plant matter for next year's food supply, i.e., your garden crops.

But you don't have to wait until fall to put a big dent in the life plans of insect pests. Insects prefer plants that are easy prey, and plants past their prime are the easiest prey of all. In our climate, most insects hatch three or more generations every summer. Getting rid of target plants — those that already have borne fruit and are too weak to defend themselves — makes it more difficult for insects to reproduce. They may leave the garden altogether in search of a better breeding place.

18

ROTATE CROPS

When you arrange your garden so that different vegetables take turns occupying the same space, it's called crop rotation. Rotating plantings helps to prevent the depletion of specific nutrients in the soil and makes it difficult for soil diseases and insects to get a firm foothold in the garden.

When harmful insects complete their life cycle, they don't just disappear. Many burrow into the soil and spend the winter quite near where they fed the summer before. If they find their favorite vegetables at their doorstep when they emerge in spring, they probably will have a better summer than you will. Also, tomatoes, eggplants, lima beans, and other popular garden plants sometimes host harmful fungi and bacteria around their roots. The safest strategy is to move these susceptible plants around in the garden, so that diseases like fusarium wilt, bacterial wilt, and others have only a little time to get established before their host plants are removed.

Summer insects live short, nightmarish lives. They are constantly in danger of being plucked away by birds, trapped by spiders, or having a wasp come along and lay her eggs inside them. Those that survive will cause some damage, but research has shown that many vegetables can have up to thirty percent of their leaves removed by chewing insects before yields are reduced. Unfortunately, bugs cannot count (much less compute), and they rarely stop at the thirty percent mark once they get started. It's therefore important to identify insect problems early and to treat them before their populations mushroom, as insect populations do.

Some harmful insects have special survival talents and escape the controls that nature (and gardeners) provide. These are the ones that usually demand direct treatment before the growing season is over. But they are not an insurmountable force. Whether or not you garden organically, the key to keeping the upper hand with damaging insects is early detection and timely control. Every garden pest has a weak place in its life cycle or some special susceptibility that enables you to exert your dominance — without using the most dangerous insecticides.

19

Choose the least lethal method when you're faced with a super destructive insect pest. Some of the substances I suggest may be new to you, but they do work. Even when using "organic" pesticides, remember that they are poisons and be careful with them, too. Wear rubber gloves and avoid breathing fumes or dust. If you use more potent insecticides, follow instructions precisely and never allow the chemicals to come in contact with your skin.

SOUTHERN INSECTS: THE MOST UNWANTED LIST

APHIDS

These tiny summer insects emerge in May and remain in the garden all summer. They are a serious problem only when they are colonized by ants; the ants herd them around like cowboys herding cattle. Aphids suck juices from plants and some carry bacterial and viral diseases. They are happiest in hot, dry weather. A spray made of plain water and a few drops of liquid detergent is usually effective in chasing them away. Very small colonies on field peas, okra, and other heat-tolerant vegetables do not reduce crop yield.

BLISTER BEETLES

These large insects may grow up to three-fourths of an inch long. They are black with yellowish stripes, and they feed on potatoes, tomatoes, eggplants, beans, and other crops, in that order. Blister beetles leave behind noticeable blobs of black excrement, and they often feed in groups. In pre-pesticide days, Southerners "swept" blister beetles out of their gardens with freshly cut cedar branches. If you catch them early, you can handpick them, but don't squash them with your fingers — their body fluids may cause a blister (hence the name). If they appear in very large numbers, dust or spray with rotenone (a plant-derived insecticide with a half-life of only a few days), and then do it again in three days for good control.

20

INSECTS: THE MOST UNWANTED LIST

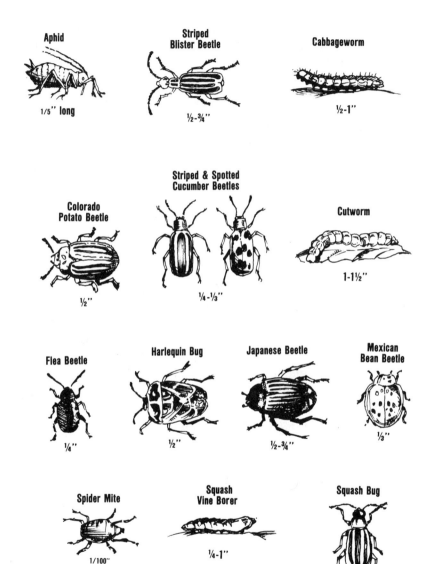

Aphid
1/5" long

Striped Blister Beetle
½-¾"

Cabbageworm
½-1"

Colorado Potato Beetle
½"

Striped & Spotted Cucumber Beetles
¼-⅓"

Cutworm
1-1½"

Flea Beetle
¼"

Harlequin Bug
½"

Japanese Beetle
½-¾"

Mexican Bean Beetle
⅓"

Spider Mite
1/100"

Squash Vine Borer
¼-1"

Squash Bug
¾"

CABBAGEWORMS

Frequently called green cabbageworms, or loopers, these velvety green moth larvae eagerly devour all brassicas — cabbage, broccoli, collards, etc., as well as some other leafy vegetables. Bacillus thuringiensis (sold as Dipel or Thuricide) will eliminate them. Bacillus thuringiensis, often abbreviated as B.t., is harmless to humans but kills many soft-bodied chewing insects like cabbageworms. For good control, you should spray every week or so, for the moths lay eggs continuously from April to October. However, late summer and fall populations generally are sparse, since summer grasshoppers feed on the parent moths. Birds consider these worms a great delicacy, so encourage them to feed near infested vegetables.

COLORADO POTATO BEETLES

Local folks call these potato bugs, or sowbugs, and are they ugly! They do most of their damage while in the larval stage, though adult beetles feed for awhile in early spring before they lay their eggs. Fully grown beetles have vivid yellow and black stripes down their backs, and they lay their eggs on the undersides of potato leaves. When the eggs hatch, the larvae (reddish-orange, soft-bodied bugs with black spots on their sides) begin eating potato leaves, and they delight in finding open blossoms — a favorite sowbug treat. Bacillus thuringiensis (see cabbageworms) gives pretty good control when the larvae are very small, but the simplest way to control them is to handpick the bugs at least every other day. Planting potatoes with or alongside beans also helps. If you can catch the adults before they lay eggs, control will be much simpler. Eggs hatch continuously through May and June, so don't stop looking for them after you've gotten rid of them once.

CUCUMBER BEETLES

These guys are awful, and nothing you can spray will get rid of them completely. As with other bugs, part of the problem is that they reproduce continuously all summer, and by August cucumber beetle populations are very large. There are two types — striped ones and spotted ones. Both are bright yellow, about the size of lady beetles, with black stripes or spots on their backs. The spotted ones grow to be larger than the striped ones. Both types feed primarily on cucumbers, melons, and other cucurbits. The tiny larval worms get inside plant roots and stems, usually just below the soil, and eat them away from the inside.

It helps to interplant just about anything among target crops, and radishes have a reputation as an effective repellent plant. You also can trap cucumber beetles by painting a board yellow (the color of cucurbit flowers) and smearing it with something sticky — honey, glue, or Tanglefoot. Douse the plants with a fine spray of water, and the bugs will fly; then you can catch them with the sticky board. Rotenone will not eliminate cucumber beetles but will kill most of the younger ones. Cucumber beetles transmit bacterial wilt, a serious problem for cucurbits in the South. Fortunately, researchers hope to offer a safe control for these critters in the next few years, with a substance derived from a certain Indian tree. For now, it's realistic to keep them only at manageable levels by using organic methods. I don't recommend using it, but malathion will get rid of cucumber beetles if you're desperate. It's a complex organophosphate, which is *highly toxic* until it breaks down. Allow two full weeks for this to occur, and wash vegetables from sprayed plants very thoroughly before eating them.

CUTWORMS

Cutworms include the larvae of more than two hundred species of moths. The worms live in the ground and eat green plant material. They are most active in early spring, when they come out at night and chop down tender young seedlings. Water helps drive them toward the surface for easy handpicking, and birds pluck them from the soil whenever they can. Tilling the soil in the fall and leaving it exposed for a few weeks helps the birds to do their job.

You can protect spring-planted seedlings by setting cutworm collars around them. The collars prevent the worms from being able to burrow up to the seedlings and cut them down.

Collars can be made of strips of cardboard or hollowed-out tin cans pushed an inch into the soil around young plants.

FLEA BEETLES

These tiny black hippity-hops do their dirty work in the heat of the summer. They love hot, dry weather, and reproduce continuously from early summer until fall. Flea beetles feed on many garden crops, leaving numerous tiny holes in the leaves. They will completely annihilate eggplants if allowed to do so. Discourage them by spraying plants with water regularly during dry periods, and by removing dead plants from the garden promptly. Eggs are laid on old plants or weed foliage. If too many flea beetles take up residence in the garden, periodic applications of rotenone in July will keep them at tolerable levels.

HARLEQUIN BUGS

Sometimes called calico bugs, these insects pose occasional problems in Southern gardens. Most of the time, there are so few of them that controls are unnecessary, but gardeners in woodland areas may catch them eating collards, potatoes, turnips, and other crops. The adults are almost a half-inch long with colorful black, red, and/or yellow mosaic patterns on their backs. They hibernate in dead plant material, so fall maintenance is very effective in controlling them. If problems become serious, dust or spray with pyrethrum — a potent plant-derived insecticide which also is used by veterinarians to treat severe cases of fleas.

JAPANESE BEETLES

In a wet summer, Japanese beetle populations may become so high that the beetles begin feeding on garden vegetables. Normally they prefer ripe peaches, blackberries, and other fruits, but they'll also eat corn silks and the leaves of various vegetables. These noisy, iridescent beetles emerge from the soil in mid-June and remain active through the first half of August.

In a hot, dry year, controls may be unnecessary — at least in the vegetable garden. The white, grubby larvae eat plant roots and can seriously damage lawn grasses and other plants, however.

Milky spore disease is harmless to humans yet deadly to these beetle grubs. Once the soil is innoculated, however, several years may pass before the disease becomes effective. Also, unless all of your neighbors innoculate their soil, adult beetles from other areas may fly into your garden. Extension agents sometimes help coordinate community-wide milky spore innoculations, but only in heavy peach-producing areas.

Japanese beetle damage to vegetables can be controlled by dusting the leaves of affected plants with rotenone every few days. The beetles are very mobile, and as soon as you get rid of one group, a new one may appear.

Japanese beetles are most active during midday, so apply rotenone early in the morning for best results. Some gardeners use malathion or Sevin (the least dangerous "hard" insecticides for the job) when Japanese beetles are devouring their vegetables. When the beetles zero in on corn silks, stick with rotenone, which breaks down much faster.

MEXICAN BEAN BEETLES

This is one pest you can count on seeing every year. It attacks green beans, shell beans, lima beans, and sometimes field peas. If left uncontrolled, it will skeletonize bean leaves until the plants die.

The adult beetles emerge in May. They look somewhat like red lady beetles, only they're a little larger and of a dusty, pinkish-brown color with black spots. Most years you'll see only a few of the adults before they lay eggs on the undersides of bean leaves, usually near the base of the plant. A female Mexican bean beetle may lay up to five hundred eggs in a season, so capture every adult beetle you see in early summer.

When the eggs hatch, the larvae immediately begin feeding on leaves. They are bright yellow, slow moving, spiny blobs. Toward the end of the larval period, they have white tufts of spines at their head end. Rotenone gives good control of these pests while they are in the larval stage — just be sure to get the dust or spray on the *undersides* of the leaves where the bugs feed. The dead carcasses usually stay attached after rotenone treatment and may be left alone. Repeat applications sometimes may be necessary, especially on runner beans that grow for a long time.

Populations of Mexican bean beetles peak out in late July. Bush-type snap beans planted in August for fall harvest often escape damage completely.

NEMATODES

Nematodes are miniscule worms that live in soil and plant roots. Once they enter roots, nematodes cause knots to form, which seriously hampers the plant's ability to gather, process, and store nutrients. Affected plants are stunted, pale, and fail to thrive. If nematodes are an established pest, the easiest way around the problem is to move the garden to a new site.

If moving your garden is not practical, another alternative is to give up growing vegetables for one season. Instead, plant the entire garden in a solid mass of French marigolds. Nematodes cannot live on French marigold roots and simply starve to death. For best results, leave the marigolds in the garden for the full growing season. Appropriate varieties include *tangerine, petite gold,* and *petite harmony.* Interplanting marigolds with other crops will have little effect, since almost all plants except French marigolds are hospitable host plants for nematodes.

SPIDER MITES

These microscopic insects cause serious damage only during periods of drought in midsummer. They barely can be seen, and a silvery web-type material on leaves and stems is the most obvious clue to their presence. Many predatory insects attack them, and they cannot tolerate damp conditions. Spray plant foliage with a forceful spray when watering during dry spells, especially that of eggplants, peppers, squash, and tomatoes. Remove infected plants from the garden as soon as they finish bearing. Very severe problems with spider mites indicate low soil fertility and/or too little water.

SQUASH BORERS

Damage due to squash vine borers is easily confused with that caused by squash bugs and cucumber beetles. Most of the time, the most threatening of the three pests are the borers. They are the larval worms of a fast-moving orange and black moth. The moth lays tiny eggs near the base of thick-stemmed squash and other cucurbits. When the eggs hatch, the worms immediately burrow into the stem and feed on the plant from the inside. Affected plants wilt, getting a little worse each day, and usually die within a week if left untreated. The final evidence of borer infestation is greenish-yellow gunk, or "frass," coming from open sores along the main stem of a suffering plant.

Planting early is a good way to escape borer damage, since the plants have plenty of time to produce before the borers get to them in June or July. A more innovative solution is to wrap the plant bases loosely with cotton gauze, which prevents the moths from attaching their eggs in the first place. Insecticides are ineffective against squash borers, since the stem protects the worms from contact with externally applied poisons. However, an unusual treatment that works is to inject Bacillus thuringiensis (see cabbageworms) into the hollows of squash stems, but this must be done while the borers are very young. I wait until the first squash plant shows signs of borer damage before giving all my other plants a B.t. vaccination. Once the borers are actively feeding, they may be surgically removed, provided you get to the plants before the borers have caused the stems to start rotting. Slit the stems lengthwise with a sharp knife and carefully pull the worms out with tweezers.

A similar larval worm, the pickleworm, also attacks cucurbits, but it attacks the fruits rather than vines and stems. Pickleworms often enter from the ground, so damage can be prevented by laying a piece of folded newspaper between ripening fruit and soil.

27

SQUASH BUGS

The best way to control squash bugs is to catch them on the run. The adults are about a half-inch long, brown, and look like a slender "stink" bug. Squash bugs emit a spicy, peculiar odor when crushed. The shells of the adults are brittle, and a common species has an orange back covered by a set of reliable brown wings. They damage all of the cucurbits, especially cucumbers and melons, which run along the ground. You also may see them on tomatoes and other crops. They do little or no damage unless they're in the cucurbit patch.

Adults emerge from winter hibernation in soil and plant debris in early June. They then spend a few days beneath cucurbit leaves in search of a mate — an obsession with squash bugs. Spray the plant foliage thoroughly with water, and the bugs will climb to the tops of the leaves, where they may be hand-picked easily. If left uncontrolled, they lay clusters of shiny brown eggs on both sides of cucurbit leaves. Gently rub the eggs to remove them. Larvae hatch in about a week and feed by sucking the juices from leaves and stems.

Rotenone is an effective control for squash bugs in the larval stage. The rest of the time, handpicking is the best control. Periodic dusting with wood ashes also helps to discourage squash bugs and other cucurbit pests.

USING INSECTICIDES

Besides the pesticides I've already mentioned (Bacillus thuringiensis, rotenone, and pyrethrum), there are about a dozen other major insecticides which are approved for use on garden crops. Most organic gardeners avoid using these "hard" insecticides, since the toxins are so strong and non-specific that numerous soil organisms and beneficial insects are killed along with the pests. Additionally, there is a longer wait from the time synthetic insecticides are used until the vegetables can be eaten safely. I manage to do without these chemicals in my garden, though I acknowledge that this is, in many cases, more of a personal decision than a practical one.

Not everyone feels this way. Many gardeners use organic methods whenever possible, but use hard insecticides to control unusually severe insect attacks. In this situation, I strongly recommend opting for the least toxic products available to do the job. Malathion, an organic phosphate insecticide, is popular since it is highly effective on a number of pests, disappears relatively quickly, and is safer to handle than many other insecticides. Sevin, the trade name for cabaryl, is more toxic than malathion yet less dangerous than many other products. Sevin is toxic to honeybees and therefore should be used to treat only specific insect infestations. Routinely applying any pesticides, including the natural ones, is a very bad idea. The natural balance between good and bad insects is destroyed, and harmful insects may become totally unmanageable.

All of the leafy vegetables are poor candidates for pesticide treatment. The chemicals become trapped in small leaf crevices and may never wash away completely. When other vegetables are sprayed or dusted with insecticides (including the natural ones), *always* wait the recommended number of days before picking and eating the vegetables. Read the package label of all pesticide products carefully and take every suggested precaution before handling the product.

DISEASES OF GARDEN PLANTS

All garden soils host a broad array of bacteria, fungi, and other microscopic life forms. Most of these organisms are either beneficial or harmless, but a few of them can be devastating to garden crops. These troublemakers commonly are referred to as "diseases," and they are a signal that something serious has gone amiss in the garden. Oftentimes the cause can be traced to long spells of cool, wet weather, poor soil drainage, or use of contaminated seeds or transplants. Unquestionably, the best strategy against garden diseases is prevention. Most of the gardening methods that improve soil quality and plant vitality also help to prevent garden diseases.

Following is a checklist of things to do to strengthen your garden's resistance to disease:

1. Select a sunny, well-drained location as the garden site. Many diseases need mucky conditions in order to get a foothold. Plant in raised beds if drainage is a problem.

2. Remove failing plants and debris from the garden during the growing season. Infected plant foliage left on or near the garden's surface can carry diseases over from one year to the next. Bury crop residues or compost them.

3. Rotate crops so that organisms which require the presence of particular host plants will have a hard time finding them.

4. Space plants far enough apart so that air can circulate freely through the leaves and stems.

5. Keep fruit and leaves from coming into direct contact with the soil by mulching around the plants and/or staking them up.

6. Use uncontaminated seeds and transplants. Seeds grown in the relatively dry, disease-free climate of the western United States are preferable. Whenever possible, grow your own seedlings.

7. Grow resistant varieties, especially when disease problems are evident.

8. Make sure that plants are adequately fertilized. Struggling plants are much more susceptible to diseases than healthy ones.

9. Keep weeds and insects under control. Many viral diseases are transmitted by insects.

IDENTIFICATION OF COMMON GARDEN DISEASES

Downy mildew and *powdery mildew* are fungal diseases common on beans, garden peas, squash, cucumbers, and melons. Upper sides of affected leaves have white, powdery growth. The fungi thrive when rains are frequent and daytime temperatures do not exceed seventy-five degrees. Treatment includes planting in raised beds to improve drainage, delaying planting until weather warms up, and wide spacing to improve air circulation.

Rust fungi attack beans and corn. The symptom is small, reddish-brown, raised spots on leaves. Cool, wet weather contributes to the problem, as do contaminated seeds and transplants. Use rotations religiously if rust is present anywhere in the garden.

Fusarium wilt soil fungi affect tomatoes, sweet potatoes,

cabbage, beans, and other vegetables. Plant resistant varieties and keep transplants healthy. Root damage of any kind increases risk.

Early blight is caused by fungi which are active during damp, mild weather. Lower leaves of affected plants have dark, circular spots. Poor garden sanitation and lack of attention to rotations contribute to the problem. Plant tomatoes and potatoes far enough apart so that air can circulate freely throughout the plant foliage. *Late blight* is a similar disease which occurs in fall when temperatures become moderate.

Southern blight fungus attacks tomatoes, peppers, and several other vegetables. Infected plants wilt and die, usually in small groups, during periods of warm weather. The fungi live on plant debris of all kinds. Santitation and crop rotation are excellent controls.

Black rot is a serious bacterial disease of brassicas, but requires warm weather to get established. Grow target crops only during cool weather and compost the plants after harvest.

Cucumber mosaic and *squash mosaic* are viral diseases that are spread to cucurbits by aphids and cucumber beetles, and can be sustained by certain weed hosts. Remove affected plants immediately. If either of these diseases has been identified, do all you can to keep weeds and insects at minimum levels.

Rx FOR GARDEN DISEASES

It's much easier to prevent garden diseases than to effectively cure them. Various chemical fungicides that will get rid of some diseases are available, but there are several problems inherent in using them in the home garden. First, these chemicals are most effective if they are applied *before* the diseases are well established. Second, they often must be applied frequently so that a film of fungicide continuously covers the plants. Many fungal diseases attack during periods of rainy weather, which means that the fungicides must be reapplied after every rainstorm to be effective. Also, remember that whenever fungicides are applied, non-destructive soil fungi are killed, too. I think that chemical fungicides aren't really appropriate for the home

31

garden, and are best used only by commercial growers who use them to insure the success of their crops (and their livelihoods).

Instead of using chemicals to control diseases, pay attention to the many ways you can effectively prevent their occurrence in the garden. As a first-aid measure, you might try dusting susceptible plants with fixed copper (or copper bordeaux) during periods of mild, rainy weather. This is the only "organic" fungicide, and like the most sophisticated chemical agents, it's most effective when applied before diseases become established. If you opt to use chemical controls such as Maneb or captan, check first with your local Extension Service to make sure you choose the right "medicide" for the disease you want to bring under control. Use such products as carefully as you would any other agricultural chemicals, and always read the label before you remove the cap.

As gardeners, we are continually manipulating the environment so as to steer things in our favor — by enriching the soil, by replacing nature's weeds with plants we prefer, and by going a step higher in the food chain and altering pest populations. The role we occupy in the garden system is that of caretaker and guardian, and as such, there are many things within our control.

Even so, we are not the most powerful force in the garden. That title belongs to the weather.

4

THE SEASONS
OF THE GARDEN

There are two things about Southern weather which are obvious — it's hot and it's humid. Beyond that, I could mention that winters usually are mild, that we get a good bit of rain, and that spring and fall are the most pleasant times of year to work outdoors. Simple statements, right? Yet these basic weather factors, more than anything else, control the design of a good Southern garden. Understanding how our long growing season can best be divided up into "vegetable" seasons, and getting acquainted with which crops should be planted *when* are basic skills for the Southern gardener. But before a garden can be called successful, you have to do well growing the vegetables you like to eat *and* not kill yourself doing it. Both can be accomplished by putting the whole gardening year to work — not just parts of it.

To clarify how this works, I'll divide the growing season into manageable pieces, suggest seasonal checklists of gardening activities, and discuss the impact seasonal weather trends have on the vegetable garden. But first let's look at the South's climate for a moment — the big picture of how things work in nature.

Temperatures slide up and down as the seasons change. However, the length of day, the slant of the sun, and the amount of humidity are often just as important to garden plants as daily temperatures. Each vegetable you grow already carries with it a defined genetic program for when and how it will grow, and much of that program is linked to small seasonal changes in the weather. Genetically speaking, some plants are strangers to the environment they find themselves in, having been brought here only a few generations ago. Of these "imported" plants (which include almost everything in the garden except beans, squash, and primitive grains), most like it fine here and do well by growing vigorously during whatever *part* of the growing season they find most appropriate. To get the most from a food garden, the first step is to learn where your favorite vegetables fit into the growing season — whether at the beginning, the middle, or the end. The second step is to learn how to cultivate and take care of your plants, so that they can do what they do best — grow.

For Southerners, this can get very complicated, since we have a long growing season and consequently are faced with the task of succession cropping. Not succession planting (re-planting the same vegetable two or three times, several weeks apart, in order to get a long harvest,) but succession *cropping* — growing one vegetable followed by another, and possibly even a third one, in the same garden space and in the span of one growing season. It's only through succession cropping that we can grow a varied selection of vegetables — the same vegetables we'd most likely buy if we didn't grow them ourselves.

In a productive garden that's designed for *eating,* the growing season stretches far beyond the average dates of the first and last frosts. In such a garden, several cold-hardy plants should be growing vigorously before the last frost in spring. When the first killing frost comes in fall, there should be a dozen crops awaiting the arrival of those ice crystals — plants like collards and spinach that need frost to improve their flavor. To take a closer look at what our climate invites us to do in our gardens, let's look at a fully developed gardening year.

WINTER
(December — February)

Things To Do:
- Plan the garden and order seeds.
- Make compost and collect organic fertilizers.
- Start cold-hardy seedlings indoors.
- Harvest winter vegetables.

34

GARDEN PLANNING

Around the first of each year, just as the post office people recover from Christmas, the seed catalogs arrive. I think it's a good idea to collect several seed catalogs. Even if you don't order much, seed catalogs help you to discover what's new from the top plant breeders and provide access to vegetable varieties you can't find locally. Most winter gardening chores are not that exciting (for example, turning the compost heap), and the inspirational pictures that jump from the pages of seed catalogs are good for your gardening spirit.

Begin planning the coming year's garden right after the New Year. The garden plan doesn't have to be elaborate, but it should encompass a few basic requirements. The most important consideration is to select the vegetables that you and your family most like to eat. It's silly to waste time and garden space on crops that have a slim chance of being appreciated once they reach the dinner table. Few people are so blind that they plant crops that no one likes, but most of us tend to over-plant the easiest crops, which subsequently go to waste. Examples are radishes, zucchini, lettuce, turnips, and mustard greens. A few square feet of these are usually plenty, but since they grow like weeds, some of us get carried away.

Good planning helps to avoid these kinds of kinks. So after you choose the vegetables that are most valued at your house and estimate how much space each will require, start mapping out a garden plan. I think it's smart to fill up three-fourths of the garden with family favorites and to use the remaining space to experiment with new vegetables and varieties. By making your plan early in the year, you have plenty of time to prepare planting sites.

Garden planning would be much simpler if garden space did not need to be rotated from year to year — a must in most Southern gardens. Rotation means arranging things so that different vegetables take turns occupying the same space. The purposes of space rotation are to prevent depletion of specific nutrients in the soil and to make it difficult for soil diseases and insects to get a firm foothold in the garden. See page 19 for further discussion of crop rotation.

PLANTING CHART

	Indoors	Cold Frame (1) Cloche (2)	Transplant	Sow in open soil
J a n	celery onions herbs cabbage	celery (1) parsley (1)		
F e b	broccoli cabbage herbs	broccoli (1,2) cauliflower (1,2) kohlrabi (1,2) celeriac (1) onions (1) lettuce (2)	cabbage asparagus	onion sets
M a r	eggplant peppers tomatoes	kohlrabi (1,2) lettuce (2) beets (2) artichokes (1)	broccoli cabbage cauliflower kohlrabi onion plants herbs	sweet peas, turnips, potatoes, spinach, radishes, carrots, beets, collards, lettuce, celtuce, swiss chard
A p r	eggplant peppers tomatoes	eggplant (1) peppers (1) tomatoes (1)	kohlrabi lettuce tomatoes	beets, radishes, carrots, chard, lettuce, beans, potatoes
M a y	tomatoes		tomatoes peppers eggplant sweet potatoes	beans, pumpkins, corn, field peas, squash, cucumbers, sunflowers, gourds, okra, melons, basil, peanuts, summer savory
J u n			sweet potatoes tomatoes	beans, sunflowers, peanuts, corn, okra, pumpkins, field peas, squash
J u l	broccoli Brussels sprouts cauliflower cucumbers celeriac			okra, field peas, potatoes, winter squash, cucumbers
A u g	lettuce kohlrabi leeks		broccoli Brussels sprouts cauliflower cucumbers celeriac	spinach, beets, salsify, squash, carrots, turnips, rutabagas, collards, sweet peas, chard, beans, kale, cucumbers, orientals
S e p	parsley		garlic bunch onions lettuce kohlrabi leeks	spinach, salsify, lettuce, collards, orientals, radishes, turnips, rye, mustard, carrots, kale
O c t		scallions (1) lettuce (1) orientals (1) collards (1) spinach (1)	garlic bunch onions parsley	spinach, rye, wheat, oats, potatoes

36

MAKING COMPOST

As explained in Chapter 1, compost is the best fertilizer you can give growing plants, and it also improves the quality of garden soil. Compost heaps which are set up in fall and turned several times during the winter usually are ready to use by mid-spring — just when it's needed most. Compost works slowly in cold weather and may freeze from time to time. Covering the heap with black plastic will help keep it warm, but don't worry if the heap doesn't heat up until spring. Repeated freezing and thawing breaks down tough plant fibers, which means the materials will rot a little faster in spring when temperatures are warm enough to promote decomposition.

START COLD-HARDY SEEDLINGS INDOORS

Some herbs, celery, cabbage, broccoli, and onions can be set out when hard freezes are still frequent. Start seeds of these vegetables indoors in flats or styrofoam cups as early as possible, so they'll be big enough to handle by the time you're ready to harden them off and set them out.

HARVEST WINTER VEGETABLES

Plan things right and your harvest of fresh vegetables will continue through the deadest season of the year. Kale, parsnips, carrots, and salsify usually can be harvested throughout the winter. Additionally, wheat, rye, and clover will stand through the cold months as cover crops. Potatoes also may be planted in the fall under a thick mulch, and will spend the winter developing long sprouts which subsequently produce incredibly large yields of spuds. The garden never sleeps.

SPRING
(March — Mid-May)

Things To Do:
— Set up a cold frame.
— Make early plantings under cloches.
— Plant cool-weather vegetables.
— Begin mulching to control weeds.

SET UP A COLD FRAME

The most common season-stretching device used to get seedlings off to an early start is the cold frame, which essentially is an insulated box with a translucent top set into the ground, forming a mini-greenhouse. Cold frames are most useful for hardening off seedlings that have been started indoors and for wind protection of young plants. I also recommend starting seedlings of tomatoes, peppers, eggplants, and other vegetables that cannot tolerate frost in a cold frame.

The frame itself doesn't have to be fancy — the sides of mine are made of scrap pieces of plywood and the top is an old doorframe covered with two sheets of heavy plastic. Always vent your cold frame extremely well. Solar heat trapped inside a closed cold frame can easily burn up tender seedlings, and too much moisture inside the frame invites fungal diseases. A safe rule of thumb is to open the frame in the morning and close it at night, even if the days are cold. As extra protection, cover the cold frame with old blankets when a late freeze threatens seedlings, such as tomatoes, which prefer more tropical conditions.

MAKE EARLY PLANTINGS UNDER CLOCHES

In late February and March, planting in open soil often means sloshing around in the mud between rainstorms, and pushing a few pea seeds into the ground. As for all those little bitty seeds that also can be planted (lettuce, turnips, radishes, carrots, etc.), sticking them in mud won't work. They either will wash away or rot. A better plan in soggy weather is to plant untransplantable vegetables like these under cloches.

A cloche is any device that offers on-site weather protection for tender plants. It must admit light so that plants can manufacture the energy they need to grow, and it also must be able to ventilate excess heat. Still, there are no hard and fast rules as to what constitutes a cloche. It can be a plastic milk carton, with the bottom cut out, placed over a small plant. Pieces of hinged plexiglass which sit over plants like little pyramids are popular cloches. But for my money, the most versatile set-up is a four-foot section of either four-inch or six-inch net or welded wire (concrete reinforcing wire), bent into an arc and

THE COLD FRAME

Keep cold frame closed in late winter except on warm, sunny days. Insulate the base by banking it with leaves, sawdust, or some other organic material. Cover the closed frame with blankets overnight to protect seedlings from hard freezes.

When days become warm, keep the cold frame open unless overnight frost protection is needed. Remove insulation to improve ventilation. Keep seedlings well watered.

CLOCHES MADE SIMPLE

Cloche entire beds with arcs of concrete reinforcing wire covered with plastic sheeting. Use pieces of wood or other weights to keep plastic in place. Leave ends open unless a hard freeze is expected.

Plastic milk cartons make excellent cloches for broccoli, tomatoes, peppers, and other plants. Remove bottom and cut a hole in the top of the handle. A slender stick shoved through the hole and several inches into the ground will keep the cloche from blowing away. Remove caps to aid ventilation. Mulch if desired.

covered with three-mil or better plastic sheeting. This type of cloche is portable, easy to repair, simple to ventilate, and secure on the ground. Once the weather warms and the cloches no longer are needed, the frames (sans plastic) make good protection over seedbeds for keeping small children, dogs, and other critters out of the lusciously soft soil. They also can be fastened into cylinders and used as tomato cages in the summertime, when the last piece of equipment you need is a heat-gathering cloche.

As with the cold frame, vent cloches so that young vegetables are not subjected to extreme heat or suffocating humidity.

PLANT COOL-WEATHER VEGETABLES

In addition to vegetables started in the cold frame and under cloches, several other crops can be planted in cold spring soil. Sweet peas and potatoes should be planted as soon as the soil becomes dry enough to work, and spring is the best time of year to start new asparagus beds. When planting these big spring crops (and when setting out transplants from the cold frame), always wait for a break between rains, and never work in cold, soggy soil. If you do, the soil will glue itself into clumps that won't pulverize once they're dry.

As the days lengthen and temperatures rise into the truly comfortable range, the most tempting thing to do is to plant and plant and then plant some more. But excessive spring planting of the wrong vegetables can be one of the worst things you can do to rob yourself of the personal pleasure of gardening. Many vegetables planted in spring will mature in the hottest, most bug-ridden part of summer — probably all at once. While I'm not saying don't plant, I am suggesting that planting too much in spring (and not enough at other times) is a common problem that can reduce the total productivity of the garden. Additionally, there are many non-traditional vegetables that grow well in our area *only* in the springtime. Cauliflower, celery, broccoli, and beets simply don't do well if not grown primarily during the months of March and April, when both the soil and the air are relatively cool.

What about avoiding insects by planting early? This

works well for a few crops, particularly squash and its relatives. However, most summer garden plants simply will not grow when the soil is still cool (beans, okra, some types of corn). It's useless to plant them too early. Use spring for growing cool-weather vegetables as much as possible, and wait until May to plant more heat-tolerant crops. Rainfall should be a little lighter by then, the days will be longer, and you'll have many more opportunities to work in warm, dry soil.

START MULCHING
Mulches applied to the soil surface in late spring are the most effective way to reduce problems with weeds for the entire growing season. Mulches also keep the soil beneath them cool and moist, just the way brassicas, lettuce, and other cool-weather vegetables like it. Leave areas to be planted with beans, tomatoes, and other summer crops unmulched so that the soil can be warmed by the sun.

SUMMER
(Mid-May — August)
Things To Do:
— Plant hot weather crops.
— Harvest vegetables planted in spring.
— Water as needed.
— Take a break.
— Start planting fall crops.

PLANT HOT-WEATHER CROPS
Early summer (May and June) marks the end of the first planting season of the year. There are only a few vegetables that do well when planted just as summer is getting under way: field peas, okra, sweet potatoes, peanuts, watermelons, and sturdy tomato plants. Most other vegetables planted at this time of year are either eaten by insects or wilt to death when daytime temperatures hover in the nineties. The plants named here and on the planting chart on page 36 have little, if any, trouble with hot, dry weather. Plant them fearlessly through the end of June.

HARVEST VEGETABLES PLANTED IN SPRING

Vegetables that are already in the ground when the weather gets hot will either deteriorate and die (lettuce, brassicas, early squash) or else they will rapidly approach maturity (corn, tomatoes, beans). The long days cause vegetables to ripen fast. In midsummer, it's important to pick all vegetables as soon as they ripen, both to get them at their peak and to encourage the plants to send their energy to underripe specimens. If you plan your garden right, picking perfect vegetables will be your most frequent summer chore.

WATER AS NEEDED

The stress that garden plants withstand on hot summer days is severe. Leaves curl up in midday, when roots can't pump enough water to them to keep the cells filled. Plants actually may burn in the midday heat if a dry heat wave hangs on too long. Your protective instincts may tell you to water, but it's best to hold off as long as you can, particularly during the long dry spell of the summer. The longer plants go without rain, the deeper their roots will reach in search of water.

It's finally time to water when leaves that wilted the day before are still drooping the next morning. At this point, you need a soaker hose. You can buy one, or you can make one out of that piece of hose you ran over with the lawn mower last summer. Put a cap on one end and a male coupler on the other, and punch small holes down the length of the hose. Snake the soaker hose around the places you want to water, so that water will drip from the holes into the soil around plant roots. This is the best way to water in midsummer, because water flows into the soil at a rate the soil can accept and percolates very deeply, and little water is lost to evaporation. Also, you can turn the soaker hose on and forget about it for an hour or so. Best of all, when you water well, you don't have to water often. Even when rainclouds pass you by for weeks at a time, deep watering once a week (combined with the use of mulches) should supply sufficient water for any garden crop.

TAKE A BREAK

When the weather gets really hot, don't start feeling like a failure if your tomatoes, peppers, green beans, and eggplants stop producing for awhile. The problem is not you, but that very hot weather causes these and other plants to "check" their own growth for self-preservation purposes. For example, tomatoes seem to know that if they set fruit, they may kill themselves trying to pump out enough water to make the reproductive effort successful. So they drop their blossoms before they can get fertilized. Then, when temperatures moderate a little, they start producing again. This midsummer siesta is called *heat check*.

Not all vegetables do it, and new, heat-tolerant varieties are being developed all the time. But for some plants, the summer heat is so intense that they just die. Once they're past their prime, beans, leafy crops, squash, some herbs, and all cool-weather crops suddenly become targets of all kinds of problems — insects, various rotting diseases, and even birds. This is the natural way death comes to plants. They become weak, their natural enemies attack them, and they die. As a gardener, you need to do what you can to keep this bug-bait out of the garden. When summer turns cruel, remove spent plants at the earliest possible time, and even destroy healthy ones if insects attack them too voraciously. Strong, vigorous plants are able to do a certain amount of defending themselves on their own, but once any plant starts to fail, it's best to take no chances. Remove it.

Both you and the garden deserve a break in the middle of summer. Southern gardens, especialy large ones, are very hard to keep up with in midsummer, when the weather is so hot that it's actually dangerous to do heavy outdoor work. You can suffer a heat stroke with weeding, hoeing, and digging in the hot sun. Short of that, your disposition and overall energy level may suffer severely from too much field work. Perspiration doesn't dry as fast when it's humid, so you *feel* hotter, too. And your lungs work harder when the air is hot and damp. Most experienced Southern gardeners get up at daybreak on summer mornings and do their garden chores then.

START PLANTING FALL CROPS

Fortunately for us, summer lasts a long time in the South, and in late summer there are enough warm days left to get in a second crop of many garden vegetables. In August, the usable growing season is just reaching the halfway point, and it's time to start planting again.

But planting in the hot soil of late summer is quite different from planting in spring. Rain tends to be scarce, and when it does rain, the sun evaporates moisture from open soil at an amazingly fast rate. To give seeds the best chance of making it, soak them in plain water for a few hours and then plant them a little deeper in the soil than you would in spring. These two steps help to insure that the seeds will have the moisture they need to germinate, which increases your chance of getting a good stand of seedlings. Unlike spring plantings, those made in late summer *must* reach maturity before hard freezes commence. Because of this time limit, you often don't get a second chance at planting and need to make sure that seeds sown in August do, indeed, come up.

Large seeds like peas and beans have no trouble pushing through a thin, water-retaining mulch of grass clippings or sawdust, but small seeds should be watered daily until they come up, and then every few days or as needed. Use a fine spray to keep from compacting the soil. To help get their summer-planted seeds up, some people cover seedbeds with damp burlap bags for the first few days after planting. You also can shade seedbeds with tree branches, old window screens, or canopies made of lightweight cloth tied between stakes.

Sturdy seedlings are easier to care for in late summer than germinating seeds. Broccoli, cauliflower, Brussels sprouts, and other transplantables for fall harvest do best when started indoors. After they have been moved to the garden, mulch to keep the soil relatively cool and treat them to a weak liquid fertilizer solution. The easiest way to do this is to punch a few small holes in the bottom of a plastic milk jug, fill it half full with a weak fish emulsion solution or manure tea, and set it down next to the plant to drip.

FALL
(September — November)
Things To Do:
- Plant fall vegetables.
- Clean up spent summer crops.
- Protect plants from frost.
- Mulch or plant cover crops.

PLANT FALL VEGETABLES

Except for the usual shortage of water, fall gardening in the South is a dream season. Most of the harmful insects are gone, or they're outnumbered by beneficial insects, like praying mantises and assassin bugs, which are most active late in the season. Still, fall gardening is a new thing for many Southerners. Turnips, collards, and other greens are traditional sowings for Labor Day, but many other vegetables find autumn in the South to their liking. Carrots, Chinese cabbage, and kohlrabi do very well, and lettuce actually grows better in fall than in spring, because there are fewer slugs around to bother it. Additionally, short season vegetables like bush beans and some squashes have just enough time (with none to spare) to produce a good crop when planted in late summer or early fall. The key is to get them planted on time.

If you're new to fall planting, you'll notice a dramatic change in the way some plants grow compared to how they perform in spring. Since the days are getting shorter instead of longer, many plants grow more slowly the older they get — just the opposite from the way things go in spring. What this means to the gardener is that most plants will take longer to mature. When considering the maturation times listed on the seed packets, always add two or three weeks if the vegetable is planted for fall harvest.

Some vegetables are real naturals for fall and don't seem to care that the days are getting shorter. Fall planted parsley, garlic, onions, kale, and spinach seem oblivious to it all. If given sufficient water, they will grow throughout the fall, then slow down for the winter, followed by a spurt of vigorous growth at the first sign of spring. It's safe to plant these vegetables as late

46

as Thanksgiving, except for kale, which needs more time to grow before days get too short. The others may be considered as pre-planted spring crops, though they actually do sprout and grow a little during the winter. In late fall, it's also time to plant sprouting potatoes under a thick mulch, which will save you valuable time in spring.

CLEAN UP SPENT SUMMER CROPS

This chore is easy to neglect ("I'll wait for a cool day"), allowing new generations of harmful insects to breed in the garden. Why invite pest problems just because you want to keep some half chewed-up plants? It's one thing to be vigilant about insects and keep suspicious populations controlled. It's quite another to hold onto badly damaged plants, whose yields will be measly at best. That's playing with fire. Send these martyrs to the compost heap when they need it. It's the one place where they may do some good. Insect problems with fall plantings often can be eliminated entirely if failed crops are removed from the garden promptly.

PROTECT PLANTS FROM FROST

Sooner or later, winter inevitably comes, and with it comes frost. While some winter vegetables have the ability to freeze over and over again without going mushy, plants with high percentages of water in their leaves cannot cope with frost. Plant foliage is damaged by frost when the liquids within the cells freeze, expand, and burst cell walls. Some plants (tomatoes, watermelons, potatoes) will blacken and die after only a hint of frost. But many other vegetables tolerate frost quite well, as long as they can adjust to it gradually. This hardening-off process, as it's called, describes the tendency of many plants to develop certain elasticity within the cells that enables them to swell and contract with the ice crystals. Scientists recently have discovered that microscopic bacteria on the leaves of tender plants actually promote the formation of ice crystals.

Plants cannot harden themselves off overnight, and even cold-hardy plants will succumb to a freeze if it comes on very suddenly. When the weather cools gradually, however, growth will continue for weeks or even months beyond the first frost — at least for cold-hardy vegetables. The process of hardening off is analagous to the right way to get a sun tan. If you stay in the sun too long the first time out, you'll burn; but if you take in the rays in gradually increasing amounts, your skin modifies itself and won't burn nearly so easily. Yet when it comes to weather, there's actually little you can do to make plants harden off gradually. However, you can cover susceptible plants with sheets of plastic, so that the frost crystals form on the plastic and not on plant leaves. Old blankets also work well for overnight protection. With a little practice, you'll be able to recognize a killer, late fall storm and gather your edible goodies before they turn to mush.

Many cool weather vegetables are improved by frost, but they're damaged by hard freezes, especially those which come on suddenly. The night before the first hard freeze, flood the garden with water just before you go to bed. The water fills open channels in the soil, and its increased density causes it to freeze slower. If cold-hardy vegetables do freeze solid, allow them to thaw completely before deciding if they've been ruined. Frequently these vegetables can recover from a hard freeze if a few weeks of mild weather follow.

MULCH AND/OR PLANT COVER CROPS

One of the important things you do for your garden soil is to protect it in winter. There are two methods to choose from — mulching and cover cropping. Both reduce erosion while enriching the soil. You may find that it takes an incredible amount of mulch to cover a good-sized garden, and plenty of time to collect and spread the mulch, too. So, if you have a large garden, I think that cover crops are the easiest way to bed down the garden for winter *and* satisfy the garden's endless need for mulch materials. In small gardens, it's usually more practical to lay down a winter mulch than to grow winter cover crops.

Fall is considered *the* time to plant oats, wheat, and rye in the South. Besides keeping the soil in place, these crops also produce an early spring cutting of top-notch mulch. For a harvest of mulch just when you need it, you can cut the grains in spring before the seeds are ripe. If you like, plant large-seeded vegetables, such as beans, directly in the stubble without tilling. Most people don't wait for this mulch harvest and turn their grains as soon as the soil dries in spring, thus using the grain foliage as a green manure. Either way, grains planted in fall prevent soil erosion during the winter, produce either green manure or mulch, and go a long way toward choking out weeds. A swath of tall, green grain is also a cheery contrast with the brown tones of early spring in the garden.

Crimson clover also may be used as a cover crop, but clovers do more good for the soil if they are left in place for more than just one winter. Unlike most other clovers, crimson clover is an annual and is worth a try, especially if you suspect that your soil is very low on nitrogen (clovers are legumes).

Any mulch material is fine for covering unused garden soil in winter. Leaves are most popular since they are easy to come by, put down, and remove. The important thing is not to leave the soil exposed to the elements. If left uncovered, earthworms retreat to deeper soil levels, and some of the best soil nutrients float away during heavy rains. In short, nothing positive goes on in the dead of winter in bare soil. Don't fool yourself into believing that exposure to winter weather will kill a lot of weed seeds, either. They are much better adapted to winter survival that you can imagine

Different usable seasons mean plenty of flexibility for Southern gardeners. Some years spring plantings may produce incredible yields, then half the summer tomatoes may rot because of too much rain, and fall may bring lots of beautiful broccoli. By making use of the "off" seasons (fall and late winter), you reduce the chances of a poor crop. If you understand the climate (the world as the plants see it), you can better evaluate everything that goes on in your lively Southern garden.

5
VEGETABLE GROWING GUIDE

(An alphabetical listing of more than forty food plants, how and when to grow them, how to protect them, and suggestions on enjoying them straight from the garden.)

Artichokes

Is it odd to lead off a discussion of vegetables with a plant that few Southern gardeners have ever harvested from their own back yards? Perhaps. And yet it's not odd to want to grow the prize of gourmet cooks, the artichoke. If you live far enough south, you can do just that.

Artichokes aren't always crazy about the South, however. The heat and humidity usually are too high for them, and they respond to summer by taking a month-long siesta. Still, if you get them in the ground as soon as the soil warms in spring, keep them watered during droughts, and give them the most reliable winter protection you can dream up, you can grow artichokes.

You'll start out with seeds that look a little like cantaloupe seeds. They are vigorous sprouters — no special instructions for germination. Yet this is one of the few vegetables that I bother to start indoors and transplant later. Artichokes need every possible hour you can cram into a growing season, and a little head start in spring is a distinct advantage, especially if you want to gather buds the first year.

Artichoke seedlings set out in warm, spring soil quickly establish themselves. As long as they're handled carefully, they become completely adjusted and begin new growth within a couple of weeks. Growth of the spiny leaves continues until midsummer, then slows dramatically, and the oldest leaves (nearest to the soil) begin to break off and die. The color of the remaining leaves fades to a greyish green. In late August, when days usually begin to cool a bit, new growth again appears in the plant's center, and the color changes back to a velvety, bluish green. In September, some plants develop side shoots — a second or third stem of leaves growing from the original plant base. Occasionally a first-year plant sends up a seed head, which can be recognized instantly as an artichoke. If you get one, eat it. If you don't, not to worry. Each plant should produce between one and four chokes next year.

The most troublesome part of growing artichokes is getting them through the winter. The root and nub, or crown, must be kept alive, and they definitely are not cold-hardy. They also are prone to rot. To keep them healthy through the cold months, prune back the leaves just before the first hard freeze, and mound some sandy soil or sawdust around the base. Then mulch with a clean, dry mulch like loose hay, and top it with a sheet of plastic. Add a second layer of mulch atop the plastic. The plastic acts as a vapor barrier and protects the plants from freezing much better than mulch alone.

Another method of insulating the plants is to prune the leaves back and cover them with a cardboard box. Then cover the box with an insulating blanket of leaves. This works well in warm, damp areas where freezing temperatures are short-lived. When a period of mild weather comes, the plants can be uncovered quickly so they can dry, which keeps them from rotting.

When the plants first start coming out in the spring of their second year, they should be fertilized. An inch or two of rotted compost or manure spread over the soil is best, for these fertilizers provide the kind of time-release nutrients artichokes need. Second-year plants also need plenty of water, for they grow very rapidly. They start to flower when they've grown a bit larger than they were the previous fall. With a half dozen plants, the harvest lasts a month or more.

After the plants have finished producing, they look pooped but are still very much alive. Allow them to rest, for this is the time in their life cycle when they are most susceptible to pests, though the pests usually are limited to slugs and snails. Try to keep the root area somewhat dry without dehydrating the plant. When the weather cools, they'll regain some of their lost vigor.

Early in the second fall, you'll probably see numerous side shoots developing on each plant. The plants may be propagated by carefully cutting the shoots and planting them in prepared beds of potting soil quality — some peat moss, some sand, and some compost-rich soil. In the lower South, where fall lasts a long time, artichokes propagated from shoot cuttings have a good prognosis, since they have such a long time to develop roots before cold weather sets in. Further north, it's more practical to start seedlings every spring, since one-year-old roots, which have had an entire growing season to develop, stand the best chance of making it through an icy winter. Overly large, old roots are prime candidates for rotting.

Artichokes are an unusual plant to work with, but well worth the special effort required. Freshly cut artichokes are much more tender than those which have been held up in shipping, and if ever there were a show-off vegetable, this is it. Besides, the best way to make a home garden pay off in dollars and cents is to grow the vegetables which cost the most at the grocery store. Such as artichokes.

VARIETIES

Two varieties to try are *Green Globe* and *Grand Burre*. The second variety is reputed to always produce chokes the first year, but that's not necessarily so in the South. Try both and see how they do in your area.

Asparagus

Here is another food that's perennial — it bears year after year without re-planting. Asparagus is much hardier than artichokes and will grow throughout the South with little care. Nonetheless, many Southerners have not yet added them to their gardens, probably because two growing seasons pass before the plants are strong enough to produce spears for the dinner table. However, once they get started, a bed can last twenty years or longer. That's the deal: You plant carefully, restrain yourself from picking for a couple of years, and then harvest the most succulent spears you've ever eaten for the next two decades. Once the asparagus is established, you can even have your choice of harvesting in spring or fall.

The first decision is whether to start with seeds or roots (called *crowns*). Seeds require an extra year before they bear, but you get a better choice of variety when starting with seeds. Planting dormant roots or crowns is a more popular method, and it works well as long as you buy quality crowns from a reputable source and get them in the ground quickly.

The best time to start a new bed is in the early spring. Since asparagus stays in the ground for years, it's important to give them a good growing medium that will sustain them for a long time. You'll need compost or manure, some lime, and some energy to put behind your shovel. Planting is the hard part. Once that's done, only about one hour of easy work each winter is required to keep them robust and healthy.

In the South, asparagus crowns should be planted five or six inches below the surface in well-enriched soil. Before the roots go in, dig in compost and ground limestone, and do your best to get it distributed deeply in the soil. Once the soil is well blended, remove six inches of it and set the asparagus roots in with the crown side up. Spread the spidery roots out so they fill up the trench. A trick for increasing yields is to put a little mound of soil under the center of each crown, so that it's raised slightly higher than the tips of the roots.

To keep the roots from rotting right off the bat, refill the trench gradually. On planting day, refill it halfway. Then wait a few weeks and add the rest of the soil.

Asparagus beds usually need regular weeding during the first two years. After the first few years, weeds are much less of a problem and tend to get choked out of the bed. Asparagus ferns are feathery and beautiful — perhaps you'll decide to use the plants as a border in your yard.

The edible parts of the plant are the young shoots which poke through the ground in early spring. The reason you don't cut them for the first two years is that these are actually the growing tips of the plants, and it takes two years before enough excess shoots are produced so that cutting them won't cripple the plants. They naturally over-produce after they have been in the ground for two years.

Traditionally, asparagus is harvested in early spring when the growing tips first emerge, but you also can force spears to come up in the fall. Asparagus cannot take being cut from twice a year, however, so devoted asparagus lovers keep two beds — one for spring and one for fall.

The spring harvest comes on naturally, but fall production of spears must be forced. To do this, cut the plants back to ground level in August and let the soil become dry. Then begin watering (the idea is to fool the roots into "thinking" that it's spring). Soon shoots appear, and the harvest continues until a good freeze comes along and stops the show. The following year, let the plants grow uncut until August again, and you have a fall cutting of asparagus once more.

No matter which harvest schedule you choose, give every asparagus bed a nice cleaning and fertilizing each winter, when the plants are fully dormant. Remove any dead plant material and cover the beds with two inches of mature compost or rotted manure, and cover with leaves or straw to keep the fertilizer from washing away. In early spring, rake back the mulch to help the bed warm up, but leave the layer of manure in place. That's about all there is to growing asparagus.

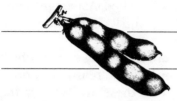 # Beans

I've never met a bean I didn't like. Most folks must agree with me, for beans consistently rank in the top three vegetables in American gardens. Because there are so many different varieties, beans are as versatile in the garden as they are on the table.

The decision of what kind of beans to plant may give you a gray hair or two since there are so many to consider. Do you want a snap bean or a shell bean? A bush type or a runner? Green, yellow, or red? If you're short on space, by all means choose climbing types, which produce a larger yield per square foot since they bear for a longer time. Try the bush types if you have space to spare. They grow faster and are easier to harvest since they bear all at once.

The rules for growing beans are simple: Grow only in warm soil, provide support if they need it, and take precautions against diseases. In the South, you also have to control Mexican bean beetles. Heat check is sometimes a problem with beans, but mulching helps to keep the plants from dropping all of their blossoms in the middle of summer. Other than this, beans require little care. Most even do well in partial shade.

The most common mistake people make with beans is to plant them too early in the spring, when the soil is cool and damp. Beans rot easily, and those that do come up in cool soil often don't do well — they never recover from poor conditions early in life. Wait to plant them until late April and May, when you know the soil is warm.

Besides their need for warm soil, all beans have another thing in common: They and other legumes (plants with "pocketbook"-shaped flowers) are able to "fix" nitrogen for themselves by hosting special colonies of bacteria in their roots. These rather spectacular bacteria convert nitrogen taken from the air into freely available nitrogen in the soil. All legumes do this, but sadly, beans are not as good at it as peas and clover. Still, they usually can crank out most of the nitrogen they need for themselves.

This means that fertilization of beans can be modest, provided the soil is in reasonably good condition to start with. If you do dig manure or compost into the bean patch, you will pick more beans; pole beans particularly benefit from good organic fertilizers, since they stay in the ground for such a long time. But if you'd rather use your precious manures on a more finicky crop than beans, a fine alternative is to decide where the beans will go in the fall and to plant that area with a green manure — winter wheat, oats, or rye. The following March, turn under the grain, wait a few weeks, and cultivate thoroughly. In another ten days, the space is ready to plant with any type of bean. The grain green manure rots quickly and supplies enough fertilization to support a stand of beans.

Most folks plant bean seeds thickly — about two inches apart. When the seedlings are three inches high, they should be thinned four to six inches apart, or eight inches in the case of lima beans, which require more space. As you thin, pull out every weed. If you have extra herb seedlings to set out, they may be just the thing for filling holes in the row or bed. The herb of choice here is summer savory, which has an ancient reputation for being beneficial to beans. However, most weeds are of no help and should be removed.

It's traditional in the South to hoe your beans frequently to keep them free of weeds, and to keep air incorporated into the soil (for nitrogen fixing, I suppose). However, research has shown that mulching is a better alternative. Mulched beans consistently out-produce unmulched ones, and they're also easier to care for. It's fine to hoe early in the season, when the soil is just warming up, but once summer begins, by all means mulch your beans. Fresh grass clippings may be used in thin layers (three inches or less), and weathered hay, leaves, and rotted chipped bark are also good mulches. The best time to mulch spring-planted beans is just before they begin to blossom.

Beans do not need large amounts of water until after they have bloomed. In fact, too much water is sometimes a problem with beans. Many bean diseases are transmitted in water droplets, so it's bad to mess around in the bean patch when leaves are wet — you inadvertently could be playing the role of a disease-spreading giant. Serious outbreaks of bean diseases are rare, but they can happen.

The big calamity that strikes your beans probably will not be a weird fungal wilt or some other disease; it probably will be Mexican bean beetles. These spotted beetles emerge in late May, but only a few appear at first. These stragglers have spent the winter in or near the garden, where they've mated. It is the larvae and young adults from this mating that wreak havoc in the bean patch.

The best strategy against this pest is early control. As soon as you see *any* beetles hanging around in the beans, pick them off. Inspect the plants twice a week for beetles and eggs, beginning when they have five or six leaves. Mexican bean beetle eggs are yellow or yellow-orange, and the larvae are bright yellow or orange slow-moving blobs that skeletonize bean leaves from the undersides. In crowded conditions, they will feed on bean pods, too. However, they won't feed if they don't exist, which is what you must accomplish through early control.

It is crucial that the first eggs be destroyed, and the best way to do this is by hand. The eggs are laid in groups on the undersides of the leaves. You either may rub them off gently, or pick the egg-bearing leaf and dispose of it. It's highly unlikely that you will find all the eggs, and sooner or later the yellow larvae will appear. Pick them off, if there are only a few of them. If your beans are thoroughly invaded by this pest, two applications of rotenone, made one week apart, should reduce the population to a manageable size.

Since beans don't like cold soil, it's difficult to avoid these beetles by planting early, but fall crops have much less of a problem with this pest. By August, the beetle population has topped out, and their natural predators (praying mantises, assassin bugs, and birds) are much more active. However, fall crops *must* be planted in July or early August, since the shortening days delay maturation of the plants. Choose bush varieties that mature fast for fall crops.

You can do everything right in growing beans and still be unhappy with your crop if you don't harvest them at the right time. Snap beans (including wax beans and pole beans) should be carefully harvested when young and tender. Use two hands when picking, especially on climbing types — it's too easy to jerk the vines from their support.

Leave lima beans on the plants until the beans within the pods swell and are quite obvious. Some limas taste bad when picked too young. Shell beans which are to be stored dry should be left on the bushes for as long as possible — either until the pods are crispy, or until dry weather ends and further on-site drying is impossible. Only fully mature beans should be dried. In wet years, shell beans sometimes ripen and promptly get attacked by insects and various moldy-looking diseases. When this happens, shell the beans, cook them, and freeze them instead of drying.

With all types of beans, chop the spent foliage into the soil as soon as you've finished picking beans. The leaves and stems rot quickly and improve soil drainage. Also, any nitrogen left in the bean roots gets safely stored in the soil. Once cultivated, allow the soil to bake in the open sun for a couple of weeks. This periodic "solarization" helps to control soil diseases.

VARIETIES

To get your beans to really do you proud, plant all types: snap beans, yard longs, limas, black beans, Italian beans, and even garbanzos. If you're just starting out, I suggest growing *Roma* or *Blue Lake* bush snap beans first. For pole snaps, try *Kentucky Wonder 191* or *McCaslan*.

The size, color, and flavor of lima beans vary according to the variety grown. Among the bush types, *Henderson* is the variety that produces small green beans that many people call baby limas. Another bush lima, *Jackson Wonder*, produces large, purple-speckled limas. *Fordhook 242* produces large white limas on big, bushy plants. Limas also may be grown on poles or fences. Pole limas such as *Sieva* and *Florida Speckled* resist drought and insects very well.

Beets

Some people think they're not *supposed* to like beets, so they refuse to eat them. But give them a try; they're really quite good.

Besides the colorful roots, beet greens are very good, too. When cooked, they have a texture unlike any other green and a smooth, mild flavor. They don't taste much like beets at all, and they're as good as, if not better than, turnip greens. Young leaves also make nice additions to salads, or you can use them as garnishes.

I have one or two more comments to make in defense of beets. The most common criticism I hear from non-devotees is that beets taste like dirt. I admit that they do have a slight earthy taste, though this taste disappears almost completely when they are properly cooked. Other people don't like the color; these folks should try yellow beets, which don't bleed and make a mess as red beets do.

Whether you grow them for leaves, roots, or both, you'll get a better beet crop if you prepare a soft planting bed by adding rotted leaves, compost, and other organic matter to the soil ahead of time. Sandy soil which has been limed is ideal, but just about any fertile soil will do. Beets are not wild about acidic soil, and wood ashes sprinkled over the bed from time to time help to adjust things in their favor.

Beets thrive during cool weather and may be planted in early spring and again in the fall. They are very cold-hardy and will germinate even when frost is frequent in early spring. For a fall crop, plant in mid to late August, and keep the seedbed moist until the seedlings emerge. Even if you love beets, remember that most people don't, so plant only a few square feet of them at a time. Keep weeds out of the seedbed — beets just can't compete with them early in life. Thin the seedlings to three to four inches apart, and reseed bare places if needed. Later, when the leaves get large and shade the soil beneath them, a few weeds won't matter.

Gather tender young leaves when they're about four inches long. Pick only a few leaves at a time from each plant if you want to grow big roots. The roots begin to swell about two months after planting, but they don't get big overnight. Harvest small ones when they are the size of a ping-pong ball, and allow others to reach baseball size, or even larger. If left in the ground too long, however, beet roots will become tough and taste pasty.

Once you pull them up, cut off all but an inch of the leaf end. Raw, unpeeled beets keep well in the refrigerator for a month or more, or you can eat them the same day you harvest them. Scrub the roots with a vegetable brush or an old toothbrush before cooking. Then boil them in plain water for approximately fifteen minutes. The skins then will slip off easily, and the beets are ready to use in any recipe you care to try. I suggest slicing them into a quart jar and covering them with a mixture of beet juice, honey, or sugar to taste, and a few whole cloves.

Keep the jar in the refrigerator. These beets are best when marinated for two to six days.

VARIETIES

The three leading varieties of round, red beets are *Early Wonder, Ruby Queen,* and *Detroit Dark Red.* All three mature in fifty to sixty days. *Cylindra* is an unusual variety that develops a long, cylindrical red root, rather than a round one, so that you get more uniform slices. *Burpee Golden Beet* is yellow instead of red, yet still has a rich, smooth flavor. The tops of all beets are edible, but most people prefer the greens from *Burpee Golden Beet* and *Green Top Bunching.*

The Brassicas

(The Cabbage Family: Broccoli, Brussels Sprouts, Cabbage, Cauliflower, Collards, and Kohlrabi)

The brassicas are a large family of related food plants, the most popular of which are cabbage, collards, broccoli, and cauliflower. Kohlrabi and Brussels sprouts are included in this group, too, as well as some lesser-known relatives. Each of the brassicas likes to be treated a little differently, and yet they have much in common. They are so similar that you may want to plant several brassicas together, such as broccoli interplanted with kohlrabi and cauliflower. First, I'll go over some features common to all of the brassicas included here, and then I'll give specific cultural information for each of them.

The brassicas — or cole crops, as they're sometimes called — are not traditional favorites of Southern gardeners, but it's no longer a problem to grow any of these vegetables in our region. The problems associated with growing brassicas in the South have been solved by two major developments in horticulture.

The most important one is the availability of Bacillus thuringiensis — a bacteria which is harmless to mammals but effectively gets rid of green cabbageworms. Until B.t. came along, leaf-eating cabbageworms could not be controlled by any organic method except time-consuming handpicking.

The development of fast-maturing varieties also has been a boon to Southern brassica lovers. All brassicas are cool weather crops that need to grow *fast*. In the South, the cool growing seasons are spring and fall, neither of which lasts very long. As varieties have been developed that mature in sixty days or less, these vegetables have become more appropriate for the short periods of cool weather that we get in the South.

Even though many new varieties mature relatively quickly, it still helps to stretch the cool season by starting seedlings ahead of time and setting them out as transplants. In early spring, you can seed them directly in the garden by planting them in pre-prepared beds under cloches. This works especially well for broccoli and kohlrabi, which are pretty cold-hardy and can withstand hard freezes under a cloche. Cauliflower plants are not as cold-hardy, however, so cloche planting is risky. It's safer to start them indoors, and to harden them off for a couple of weeks in a cold frame before setting them out.

Whether started in cloches, on a windowsill, or in a cold frame, it's worth the extra trouble to start your own transplants. By growing your own, you have a much broader choice of varieties and can take advantage of the ones that mature super-fast. You also can capture the vigor of young plants and eliminate the risk that plants will be "set back," since the plants can go directly to the garden when they reach the perfect size. Brassica seedlings that have withstood temperatures below forty-five degrees for more than two weeks prior to setting out may be poor producers. Again, you can eliminate this risk by growing your own.

If the plants are ready to be transplanted before you're

ready to do it, gently move the seedlings to slightly larger cups or pots so the roots can keep growing. If you do buy seedlings, I suggest that you buy them as early as possible, then "plant" them in large styrofoam cups or similar containers, and let them harden off for at least two weeks before setting them out. When planning the harvest, bear in mind that the "days to maturity" statistic on the seed packet is an estimate, and that it really means days to maturity from the date you set your seedlings in the ground. In the case of brassicas, you can expect them to run a week or two later than the seed packet says.

The brassicas are heavy feeders, and they have a penchant for soil that's only slightly acid. This means that the area in which brassicas are grown should be heavily fertilized, and lime should be added during the preceeding fall. If the area hasn't been limed, wood ashes are a good quick-fix and should be used liberally when preparing planting sites. Besides preparing a good growing medium, you can help to meet the fertilization requirements of these vegetables by double-mulching them just before or at about the time they begin producing their edible parts. To do this, first remove all weeds, and then spread a layer of compost atop the soil (it can be rough). Water this down and cover with a layer of hay or leaves. Then dust with wood ashes, and the operation is complete. The nutrients in the compost trickle down to plants' roots when it rains, as sort of a time-release fertilizer, and the thickness of the mulch helps keep the root area cool and moist — just the way brassicas like it.

I've already mentioned B.t. as an effective control of the primary brassica pest, the green cabbageworm, but there is an even more "natural" control for these pests — sparrows. They love cabbageworms and do a reasonably good job of keeping plants clean of them. Lure feeding sparrows by providing perches near the brassicas — tomato cages or taut wire stretched above the plants work well. Help the sparrows discover the new feeding place by scattering a little bird seed among the plants every other day for a week. You'll probably be surprised at how helpful birds can be in the brassica patch, as well as in other places around the garden.

A common question is, do you have to plant brassicas

twice a year, or can you nurse plants through the summer and get them to produce again in fall, like they do up north? Many varieties of cabbage and cauliflower have the ability to "cut and come again." In other words, after you cut out the primary heads, the plants produce a second crop of smaller heads from the stem area that's left intact. It's very difficult to delay this second crop until fall, since brassicas find Southern summers so horrid. They seldom arrive in good condition, and by pushing them to do so, you take certain risks with your soil. Black rot, clubfoot, and several other soil diseases thrive around weak brassica roots. These diseases require soil temperatures between sixty and eighty degrees. If there are no struggling brassicas in the ground during the heat of summer, the risk of contracting these diseases is pretty slim, provided the soil is not already infected. Play it conservatively and experiment with coaxing second cuttings only from crops which mature early in the fall. Prevent buildup of microorganisms that might cause trouble by rotating brassicas religiously.

Blanching, which means protecting the inner head from sunlight, is mandatory with broccoli and cauliflower and helpful with cabbage. Hot sunshine brings out the worst in brassicas and can ruin their flavor within hours. As soon as the head becomes visible, gather the large leaves into a bundle at the top and tie them loosely with string. Or, you can pin them together with a wooden clothespin. Leave them like this for at least a week. When choosing varieties, you'll see many that claim to be "self blanching." This usually means that the plants grow many leaves near the head that curl over it naturally. However, this self blanching is a tendency, not a guarantee. You still should blanch manually at every opportunity.

All brassicas reach a perfect state of maturity when they must be cut, and the condition lasts for only a couple of days. If you can't make it to the garden when your brassicas are expected to mature, arrange for a brassica-sitter. When harvesting, cut or pick when slightly immature if necessary. Brassicas go downhill fast when they have to wait too long for harvest.

The overall objective in growing brassicas is to bring them to maturity as fast as possible. This involves reducing all the stresses which the plants are likely to encounter: shortage of food or water, too little root space, damping off, and extreme hot and cold temperatures. It's really not that hard. Do it successfully and you can enjoy these remarkable vegetables as the first big crops to make it to the table in spring, and the last to go down in the fall.

Broccoli

Good timing is the only secret to growing perfect heads of broccoli in the South. They demand cool weather, and without it results will be second-rate. By splitting the broccoli season into spring and fall crops, you should be able to grow most of the broccoli your family will eat in a year. Broccoli freezes beautifully, although it usually gets eaten before it makes it into storage.

Both spring and fall crops require good soil, adequate spacing, and treatment for green cabbageworms. They also must be planted as early as possible to take advantage of every available day of cool weather. Since broccoli is a "cut and come again" vegetable, the more cool weather you have after the plants have reached maturity, the more broccoli you'll be able to harvest.

SPRING

There are two ways to go about preparing for the spring crop, which will be gathered in May and early June. You either can start seeds indoors and set them out when they have six leaves, or plant the seeds directly in prepared beds. Either way, it pays to prepare the rows in fall or winter, adding whatever organic materials the soil needs to maximize its moisture holding capacity. If you wait until spring, the soil may stay too wet to cultivate, causing serious delays in getting the plants up and growing on time. If you can't prepare the bed ahead of time, reserve some of your best compost and place it in transplanting holes when the seedlings are set out.

The simplest way to grow strong, early broccoli plants is to seed them directly into well prepared beds in February and cover the beds with a cloche. As soon as the plants are up, start leaving the ends of the cloche open to harden off the plants. Broccoli can take cold temperatures, but cold spring winds twist and batter the plants severely. If grown under cloches, they gradually will become accustomed to this kind of strain. When setting out seedlings, place mini-cloches made of plastic milk cartons over each plant and remove them during periods of mild weather.

Proper spacing is important, and maturity will be delayed if broccoli is too crowded. Space the plants at least two feet apart, so that the leaves barely will touch when they are full grown. You can start out with them thicker than this and thin as they grow. Immature broccoli plants, stems, and leaves taste pretty good.

Mulch spring broccoli as soon as the plants begin growing vigorously. In between spring rains, dust the mulched beds liberally with wood ashes. The mulch helps to keep the soil cool and also enriches the soil as it decomposes. Broccoli needs all the nutrients it can get. Big plants with massive root systems grow the biggest heads and keep growing for a longer time.

When heading is to commence, the new leaves which appear at the top of the plants will be smaller than those at the plant's midsection. The first you'll see of the head will be a bumpy, yellowish-green eye at the top of the stem. It will grow rapidly, lengthening and broadening noticeably each day. As soon as you see it, blanch the large outer leaves so that no sunshine touches the head. When you can't wait any more, lop off the head with a sharp knife, cutting at an angle so rain won't accumulate in the stem. Leave the plants alone for a while after the center head has been cut. With most varieties, smaller heads will emerge from the trunk within a few weeks.

FALL

Many people have even better luck by growing their broccoli in the fall. The flavor improves remarkably when the plants mature in cool weather, and the same varieties grown in spring and again in fall probably will taste better the second time around. Fall also is the best time to grow large crops destined for the freezer.

Fall crops should be started indoors from seed in July and set out as soon as they have six leaves. Broccoli seeds will not germinate when baked in hot soil. However, you can place the flats in a shady place outdoors and then move them into stronger light when they have three leaves. If you keep your seedlings in an air-conditioned place, let them get used to the outdoor heat for a few days before transplanting them.

Days get shorter in fall, and the shortening photoperiod slows down the growth of almost all garden plants. It's therefore important that your broccoli plants be well established by Labor Day. Prevent them from being "set back" during transplanting by handling them carefully. Water with weak manure tea or some other lightweight fertilizer every few days during the first two weeks after transplanting in the fall.

The closer to maturity broccoli is when the first frosts come, the less likely it is to be damaged. Fall broccoli usually matures in late October, *after* the first freeze but before freezes become frequent. Heavy frost may burn some of the older leaves, but it should not bother the main stem. If the plants have begun to head and a freeze is expected, blanch the leaves to prevent ice crystals from forming directly on the heads. You also can cover the plants overnight with bushel baskets for added protection.

The remains of defunct broccoli plants get slimy and foul and are best removed from the garden. If left on the surface to decay, the foliage is subject to ring spot, a fungus that can spread to other healthy plants. Compost the plants when they begin to deteriorate.

68

VARIETIES

There are two main types of broccoli to choose from. The *Italian* or sprouting types first bear a medium-sized central head, which is cut as soon as it develops a full, green color. Once the central head has been cut, side shoots of small, long-stemmed heads will emerge from the main stem. Cut these little heads promptly, and the plants will continue to produce for several weeks. Good sprouting varieties include *Early Green Sprouting, Decicco,* and *Cleopatra*, which is very early.

The other type of broccoli includes most of the fast-maturing hybrids. These varieties mature all at once, and the heads are much bigger than those produced by sprouting types. Many of them do sprout after the center head is cut, but not nearly with the vigor of the *Italians*. A large freezer crop is easier to manage if the big-headed kind are grown, especially in the fall. The biggest broccoli head I ever grew came on a *Green Duke*. *Green Comet, Premium Crop,* and *Green Hornet* are also excellent representatives of this group. The seeds sprout rapidly and heads appear only sixty days after setting out.

Brussels Sprouts

Growing Brussels sprouts in the South can be done, but first you must consider the eccentricities of this very European vegetable. They are very cold-hardy; in fact, they like cold weather so much that they need more than three months of it in order to produce a good crop. This is the reason they are not recommended for spring planting in our area. We get only about two months of proper Brussels sprouts weather in spring, and that's just not enough. The sprouts turn mushy and bitter when left to mature in warm weather. Crisp, tender sprouts can be grown only in the fall. It's a realistic goal to have homegrown sprouts for the Thanksgiving table.

Start seeds indoors in early June in large styrofoam cups. As the seedlings grow, rotate them a quarter turn each day so they get even sunlight. When they have three leaves, begin watering with a very weak fish emulsion mixture. Meantime, prepare the planting site.

Dig out individual holes for the Brussels sprouts one foot square, placed two feet apart. Refill the holes with one part rotted manure or compost and two parts well cultivated soil. Dust with wood ashes and then water the holes well.

Sometime in August, there should occur a short spell of mild weather. This is the time to sink the seedlings into the prepared holes. Gently squeeze the root balls out of the cups, and try not to handle the stems at all. Set the plants in the soil only about one-half inch deeper than they were in the cups. Firm the soil around the seedlings gently with your hands. Water with weak liquid fertilizer once a week, or more often if rain is scarce. Mulch around the plants to help retain moisture, but keep the mulch pulled two inches away from the plants to prevent molds. Watch for cabbageworms, and spray with Bacillus thuringiensis if needed.

The bigger the plants grow, the more sprouts they will produce. The first sprouts to ripen are the ones at the base of the plant. As soon as these are big enough, carefully cut them from the plants. Their flavor is greatly improved by frost, so you may want to wait until after a few white nights have come and gone to cut them. It's fine to remove the leaves surrounding the sprouts as you cut them.

Autumn weather can be strange, and certain weather patterns can interrupt the healthy life of otherwise good Brussels sprouts. If subjected to a long period of dry weather, the sprouts may crack following a heavy rain. If they're used to warmish weather and it suddenly drops to twenty-five degrees with strong north winds, they may be frost burned. However, if they can harden off gradually, they can easily withstand temperatures as low as eighteen or nineteen degrees.

If winter comes early and suddenly, you may have to help

a little in this hardening off process. Begin by raking back the mulch — open soil absorbs more solar heat than mulch because it is much more dense. This heat is gradually released during the night, and can raise the temperature around the plants by a degree or two. Next, cover the plants with bushel baskets, old blankets, or plastic garbage bags. Just before you go inside to warm yourself, flood the base of each plant with lukewarm water.

The next day (or the next, depending on how long the freeze lasts) wait until midday or later to remove the covers. If the plants have frozen, they will recover much better if they thaw slowly. Sprouts which may seem hopelessly frozen in the morning may be perfectly fine in a few days.

Sooner or later, the winter weather will get to the plants, and they will stop growing. Depending on the severity of the winter, they may survive until February, at which time they may produce a few more sprouts. It doesn't hurt to experiment with wintering them, especially if the plants were still healthy when they became dormant. I usually leave a few of mine standing, but then I'm a fool for a winter garden.

VARIETIES

Jade Cross and *Long Island Improved* are the primary recommended varieties. If you run across a new variety that matures extra fast, by all means, give it try.

Cabbage

Cabbage is a very heavy feeder, it takes up a lot of space, and the heads seldom escape insect damage entirely. Add to this the fact that cabbage is always available at the store at a reasonable price and you may have trouble talking yourself into growing more than a few plants in your garden.

71

Since a lot of people do grow it, you usually can find transplants both in early spring and again in late summer, or you can grow them yourself. Cabbage, like Brussels sprouts, is very cold-hardy, and spring transplants may be set out as early as February. They require three months after transplanting before they form big heads. Those set out later than March will have poor flavor and much more trouble with pests than earlier plantings. It's better to wait until August to set out seedlings for fall harvest than to let spring planting dates slip back too far.

It should be no surprise that cabbageworms attack cabbage more voraciously than other brassicas. Cabbages are all leaves, the part of the plant the worms like best. They can feed between the leaves where you can't see them, making it hard to guess when you should wash them down with Bacillus thuringiensis. The only sure way to protect them is to spray periodically from the time you begin seeing small, white moths flitting in and out of the cabbage leaves. The moths, the mothers of cabbageworms, first appear in April and continue to be quite active for the rest of the growing season. B.t. is rinsed away by rain, so apply it frequently for good protection.

In fall, or in an unusually dry spring, half mature cabbage heads sometimes crack and split following a heavy rain. This happens when roots send up more water than the leaves can cope with. Once the damage is done, there's nothing you can do about it, but you can prevent it from happening in the first place. When that big rain you've been waiting for is finally imminent, cut around the plants with a sharp spade to sever *some* of the roots. Less water then will be pumped to the leaves.

Begin harvesting as soon as small heads form, and continue to cut them as you need them. Use a sharp knife to lop the heads off, and try to leave an inch of the stem (and the large outer leaves) intact. Provided cool weather continues for a while, the plants will produce a few small heads, which are perfect for boiling, around the stub.

72

VARIETIES

When starting your own seedlings, you can choose between regular tight-headed cabbage, red cabbage, or the frilly savoy types. *Round Dutch, Stonehead,* and *Market Prize* are dependable and disease resistant. Among the reds, *Ruby Ball* gets consistently high ratings. *Savoy King* and *Savoy Ace* are beautiful and very flavorful.

 # Cauliflower

This is one of those garden crops that you just have to baby along. Cauliflowers can't handle any kind of stress. They are less tolerant of both heat and cold than the other brassicas, and therefore require good timing and loving care. But if you pay attention to what you're doing, you can easily get two nice crops of cauliflowers each year — spring and fall.

New fast-maturing varieties make this possible. Cauliflowers like their weather cool or just slightly warm, which means you must get the transplants in the ground by mid-March in spring and by Labor Day in fall. Spring seedlings may be sprouted under cloches as with broccoli, or you can start them indoors. Like the other brassicas, they sprout dependably and are relatively easy to handle. Bear in mind that cauliflowers often do not mature as fast as the seed packets suggest, so adjust planting dates accordingly.

Don't get impatient at planting time. In the rush to get their seedlings planted, some people make the mistake of transplanting cauliflowers when the seedlings are too small. This sets the plants back by several weeks. Wait until they have six leaves, and then plant them in well drained beds which have been enriched with rotted manure or compost. Water with a weak fertilizer solution to help get them going. If cabbageworms start chewing leaves, spray with B.t. Encourage earthworms beneath the soil by covering the bed with a mulch.

About two months after setting out, start watching the inside of the plant for the pale green "button." As soon as you see it, tie or pin up the outer leaves to keep out the sunlight. See that the plants get regular water, and check the buttons every few days. They take about ten days to reach full size after they first appear.

Take no chances with letting cauliflower heads get over-ripe. When past their prime, the curds appear ricey as opposed to smooth and fluffy. Sunlight, even just a little, can change the flavor from mild to bitter. If you must delay cutting, cover the blanched plants with paper bags.

If a hard freeze comes along before your fall crop is ready to be harvested, protect the plants with bushel baskets or plastic garbage bags, and flood the soil with lukewarm water before you go to bed. Cauliflowers seldom withstand tempera-tures below twenty-five degrees, no matter what you do. If the curds of fall cauliflower are hopelessly damaged by frost, but the leaves look OK, cut the heads and continue to care for the plants. Some varieties have the ability to produce small second-ary heads after the first ones have been cut.

VARIETIES

Snow King and *Snow Crown* are highly recommended, since they mature in less than sixty days. *Alert* is another very fast variety. *White Empress* also is dependable, disease resistant, and productive.

Collards

Collards are synonymous with "greens" to many Southerners, and they're the easiest brassica to grow in our area. They tolerate heat very well, though they taste best when they have been through a frost or two. The cabbageworms don't like them nearly as well as the more tender brassicas, so growing them is relatively carefree.

Plant collards twice a year — in spring and again in fall. They are relatively heavy feeders, so spade an inch of rotted compost into the planting bed. Then sow the seeds directly in the soil, either broadcasting them or placing them in double rows at least six inches apart. Plant the seeds no more than a half-inch deep. Weed the bed at least until the plants are well established, and mulch to help retain soil moisture. Begin thinning when the leaves are the size of your hand, and eat the thinnings. Stop thinning when the plants are one-and-a-half feet apart, and start harvesting individual leaves instead. In spring, the collards will be good until warm weather turns them bitter. In fall, they'll last until cold weather freezes them.

VARIETIES

The *Georgia* variety grows very fast and is the best choice for spring plantings. Descendants of the *Vates* strain, however, are much more cold hardy and are better than *Georgia* for fall crops. *Vates* will winter over pretty well most years and produce modest picking first thing in the spring. See *Kale* (P. 101) for a closely related plant that winters over even better.

Kohlrabi

This has got to be the funniest looking member of the brassica family. Instead of getting a big head, it grows a big bottom — a delicious, round thing that may be eaten raw or cooked. I never tasted kohlrabi until I grew some, for you almost never see it at the supermarket. Now I include it in my garden twice a year, spring and fall. It is truly a gourmet vegetable and well worth the small effort necessary to grow it.

Kohlrabi is very well suited for the South. It matures in less than sixty days and makes a wonderful spring crop. Since kohlrabi grows so fast, there is some leeway allowed in planting times. Spring plantings may be started from early February to late March, followed by fall sowings from late August to mid-September. The seeds can be planted directly in the ground like collards, or you can grow them from seedlings as you do broccoli.

Although it does need its share of nutrition, kohlrabi can adjust well to weak soil. A little compost spread over the bed or buried beneath transplants is usually enough to take care of them through their short lifespan. Water them if rains are scarce, and mulch the same way you do your other brassicas.

When the plants are about a foot tall, they begin their bizarre transformation into bulbs. The base of the plant forms into a little ball, and gradually the ball gets bigger and bigger. Leaves continue to grow from the enlarged stem, and the leaves at the top become very small. Begin harvesting when they are the size of tennis balls. If they grow bigger than baseballs, they tend to get slightly fibrous, but they're still good if you cook them.

Kohlrabi is flexible when it comes to adverse weather. It doesn't turn bitter just because the days get warm, and it doesn't die back after a moderate freeze. Mature kohlrabis sometimes get frozen solid late in the fall. These still may be good, but you must let them thaw completely before cutting. Kohlrabi does not come back again after being cut.

VARIETIES

Grand Duke is more than a personal favorite. It's the fastest, juiciest, sweetest variety around, and all the seed companies have it. *Early White Vienna* is the second choice in light-colored kohlrabi. *Azure Star* has a purple skin and makes a colorful addition to the brassica patch. A mixed planting of *Grand Duke* and *Azure Star* will produce a long, steady harvest, especially in the fall. *Azure Star* requires about two more weeks of growing time, but it's also a little more cold hardy.

Carrots

Carrots are good for your eyes, your skin, and your waistline, and they are a valuable garden crop, since you can dig them fresh at those times of the year when other vegetables are scarce. Spring carrots mature at the same time as English peas, and the two vegetables are delicious when cooked together. Fall crops can be mulched over when they reach maturity and dug fresh all winter long. I suggest planting carrots four times a year — twice in early spring and twice in the fall — so that you always have them when you want them.

The flavor and overall success of carrots are determined primarily by the variety grown and not by the quality of the soil. Carrots do grow best in loose, sandy soil, but they also do well in clay with organic matter added to soften it up. For best results, plant them in raised earth beds that are no more than two and a half feet wide. Carrots must be weeded regularly by hand, and bed planting makes this easier.

Work some rotted manure into the soil, but also use leaf mold, peat moss, and other materials which don't contain much nitrogen. Carrots do need nitrogen, but if they have too much, the roots tend to branch. Potassium is what they really like, and this is easily supplied by adding wood ashes to the soil. Rock phosphate also provides many of the nutrients carrots need.

Remove any rocks and other hard obstructions from the prepared bed and rake it smooth. Then scatter the seeds thickly and bury them one-fourth to one-half inch deep. Carrot seeds germinate slowly, so it helps to pre-soak them overnight. Soaking in water that's exactly one hundred twenty-five degrees also lessens the probability of alternaria blight, but it won't eliminate it entirely. More about that later.

The seeds germinate best if kept constantly moist. Covering freshly seeded beds with damp burlap bags for a few days is helpful, especially with fall crops planted in late August, when the soil tends to be very dry. Even with extra help, carrot seeds germinate slowly and never all at once.

As soon as the feathery tops become recognizable, begin hand weeding the carrot bed at least every two weeks. Carrots are very poor competitors with weeds and will remain scrawny if you don't weed them. Avoid compacting and disturbing the soil as much as possible when weeding, and use a thin mulch of sawdust or grass clippings to discourage new weeds.

When the carrot tops are five to six inches high, it's time to start thinning them. They should be thinned to at least two inches apart, and the thinnings can be eaten. Contrary to popular belief, immature carrots are not as sweet as those that grow to full size, so don't be disappointed if the thinned-out carrots come up short in terms of flavor. The tiny, sweet carrots called "baby" carrots are a certain strain of miniature carrot.

Carrots are in peak picking condition when the tops darken to a deeper shade of green. This is your signal that the roots are complete and ready to start sending extra energy to the plant tops to help them gear up for seed production. Pull or dig after the tops darken. As more and more of them are removed and the canopy of shade is destroyed, mulch with hay or grass clippings to keep the shoulders of the remaining carrots from greening up from exposure to sunshine.

Spring crops need to be removed from the ground as soon as they reach perfection, for soil-dwelling worms will attack them once soil temperatures rise into the seventies. In fall, however, you can store your carrots in the ground until you're ready to eat them. Around the first of November (or later if weather permits), cut off the tops of full-grown carrots and go around the edge of the bed with a turning fork, loosening the soil just a little. Then cover the bed with two inches of a clean, dry mulch such as sawdust, straw, or leaves. Finally, pile plastic garbage bags filled with leaves over the bed. Provided no field mice discover them, you'll have fresh-from-the-ground carrots until they're gone.

Two soil-borne troublemakers can destroy carrot crops. The one previously mentioned, alternaria blight, is an incurable disease. If your plants do OK for awhile and then die unexpectedly, call your extension service office and ask if this disease has been reported in your area. If so, the only carrots you should plan to grow should be in pots (it really works). Nematodes also dine on carrots. Precede carrots with a season's worth of French marigolds if you suspect infestation.

VARIETIES

Medium-sized carrots that grow six to eight inches long are the ones that do best in the South. *Danvers, Nantes*, and the fatter *Chantenay* varieties are good ones to start with. *Amstel* is very flavorful and sweet, though the roots themselves are slender. This makes them a good choice for clay soils. Small, fat carrots that practically sit atop the soil also may be grown, but they must be mulched, or hot sunshine will ruin their flavor.

Celery, Celeriac, and Celtuce

You probably won't find celery listed among the vegetables recommended by your local extension service, and you may have never heard of the other two vegetables in this section. I have included celeriac and celtuce here because they are somewhat like celery and easier to grow. Celery generally is not recommended for Southern growers, since it requires more than one hundred days of cool, damp weather, and our cool seasons (spring and fall) just don't last that long. However, if you get sturdy transplants in the ground early enough in the spring, you can grow celery. Celeriac and celtuce like cool weather, too, but they don't need three whole months of it. They're not exactly like celery, but they make good substitutes and are fun and interesting to grow.

CELERY is reasonably successful when grown as a late winter to spring crop. The seeds must be started in January — the earlier the better. Celery seeds take about three weeks to germinate, but you can speed things up a bit by soaking them in warm water overnight before planting them in flats. After they sprout, either move them to a cold frame, or set them under lights so they will get enough sunlight to become husky.

Move celery seedlings to the garden when they're five inches tall, even if the weather is still cold. The plants are very cold-hardy, provided they have been hardened off. They also are very demanding of the soil and need a rich, non-acid environment that can hold water. Dig in plenty of rotted compost and leaf mold, along with ground limestone or wood ashes. Once planted, water your celery frequently. The stalks are more than ninety percent water, so they need every drop they can get.

You can begin pulling the outer stalks when the plants are

two inches in diameter. If you want big plants, blanch them by surrounding them with a very thick mulch, so that only the top few inches of leaves show. This blanching helps the plants to retain water and prevents them from greening up too much. However, it's unlikely that you will manage to grow huge plants like those you buy at the grocery store, even if your blanching operation goes perfectly. Southern-grown plants are normally on the small side, but they taste just fine. When warm weather comes, the stalks become dark, tough, and fibrous. Leave a couple of them in the ground, and gather leaves all summer for use as potherbs.

Sometimes celery yellows and dies unexpectedly. This problem is with the soil, not the gardener, and is caused by various blights. When this happens, pull up the celery and try again next year in another place.

CELERIAC is a seldom grown root vegetable which makes an excellent celery substitute, and it's very easy to grow. Like celery, celeriac requires more than one hundred days to reach maturity, and while it's growing, it looks a lot like celery. But unlike celery, the edible part of this plant is the root. Celeriac can handle warm weather and does not demand constant watering. I recommend growing celeriac as a fall crop, though it also may be planted in early spring. When grown in the fall, the roots may be left in the ground until needed, which means you can dig them fresh from the garden well into winter.

Start the seeds indoors in late July, and transplant them when they are about four inches tall and have at least three leaves. The better the soil, the bigger the roots will be, so place them in a fertile, well drained place. Water as needed until the plants begin to grow vigorously.

It's difficult for first-timers to know when celeriac is ready, since the edible part is below the ground. The best way is to count off ninety days from the date you set the plants out, or, if you feel adventurous, you can gently dig around each root to see how big it is. Celeriac roots are best when they are two to four inches in diameter. When they reach this size, dig them up, wash them off, and sample them raw. If you prefer, boil them as you would carrots, and chill them before using as a celery substitute.

CELTUCE, originally from western China, is actually a lettuce. When young, the leaves can be eaten like lettuce, though they may be too strong-flavored for some tastes. Later, when they begin to bolt (but before flower buds appear), the stalks are peeled, cleaned, and eaten like celery. Some folks say that celtuce stalks taste like cucumber.

Grow celtuce the same way you would grow spring-planted lettuce. Spring crops planted during March are the best of the year. Fall plantings sometimes do not flourish as they should, since the days are becoming cooler and shorter rather than warmer and longer. For a successful fall crop, the seeds must be planted by the end of August. Celtuce seeds sprout readily and may be sown in open soil. They are moderate feeders, so add a little compost or other fertilizer to the planting bed.

When the plants elongate into their bolting posture, it's time to enjoy the "celery" part of this vegetable. Cut the stalks, remove the leaves, and carefully remove the peeling. Then rinse under running water until the milky white juice disappears. If any bitterness is left behind, boiling for a few minutes will get rid of it.

Corn and Popcorn

It is no longer true to say that you can get really sweet corn only by eating it within minutes after it's pulled from the stalk. The sweetness genes of corn were discovered a few years ago, and since then, strains have been developed that are so sweet that they might more appropriately be regarded as fruit. Some of these new varieties have certain "everlasting" genes, which delay the conversion of sugar to starch by as much as ten days. This means that you can go to the farmers' market, buy freshly picked *Silver Queen* (the most popular sweet corn), and it will be sweet and delicious even if you don't cook it until the next day. However, roasting ears, which taste very different from sweet corn, have no fancy sweetness genes and must be cooked within an hour after they're picked.

Corn is strictly a warm weather vegetable. It's best planted in April and May. Folklore dictates that you shouldn't plant corn while wearing a jacket, so spend those last few cool, jacket days getting ready to plant. Good soil preparation before the seeds go into the ground will pay you back with more big, perfect ears later.

Corn is a very heavy feeder of nitrogen and trace minerals. It demands a lot of space and a lot of fertilizer. Country dwellers with no neighbors downwind can use chicken manure, the best fertilizer for corn. Till the soil in the fall, rake out a blanket of chicken manure mixed with sawdust (this is what you get from broiler houses), and let it sit through the winter. In spring, make shallow furrows and plant the corn. It's not necessary to re-cultivate. The chicken manure forms a thin crust that helps keep down weeds if you leave it in place.

Other animal manures work almost as well, if you don't have access to chicken manure. Your corn will like the manure best if it's put out in fall, for rotted manure has more usable plant nutrients than fresh manure. Corn, however, is seldom "burned" by fresh manure, so you can use it at planting time if you have to.

Select your corn patch carefully. In a large garden, plan all crop rotations around corn, alternating its space with legumes and leafy vegetables. In a small garden, interplant corn with squash or runner beans, preferably on the outer edge of the garden. Since corn is wind-pollinated, it should be planted in blocks rather than long, skinny rows. Very small plantings require hand pollination, so put them where you'll have easy access at tassel time.

In the South, it's risky to plant corn in hills, which heat up and dry out quickly in hot, summer weather. Plant the seeds in holes or furrows about six inches apart, and don't alert the birds — which love corn sprouts — by leaving extra seeds scattered atop the soil.

Cultivate your corn with a hoe or tiller every two weeks for the first month or so. When the plants are a foot high, thin them to fifteen inches apart and remove weeds as you thin. With hoe in hand, carefully move loose soil from between the rows and mound it up around the base of each corn plant. This will help to anchor them in place and protect them from drought. Follow up with a mulch — any mulch. All of this may take the better part of a day, but it's worth every minute. If you do it right, there will be no more work to do until picking time, and each stalk should bear two good ears of corn.

If suckers appear on the plants, leave them alone. The increased leaf area from these suckers helps the plants grow stronger, and there's no need to worry about the plants overextending themselves by trying to grow too many ears.

Sometimes you may have to lend a hand when your corn enters its reproductive phase, signalled by the emergence of the tassels. Pollen from the tassels must reach the tender silks of the unformed ears. Pollination suffers if the plants are knocked over by violent winds. Keep the stalks upright until the tassels have dropped all of their powdery pollen. If in doubt, you can hand pollinate corn by dropping pollen gathered from one plant into the silks of another plant of the same variety. During the pollination process, it's crucial that the plants have adequate water. If the silks dry out too soon, they won't be able to accept the pollen. A good mulch will prevent this from happening.

As the ears mature, certain corn pests also emerge. The most common one is the corn earworm — a caterpillar-like worm that feeds on the same part of the plant as you. A drop of mineral oil placed in the tip of each ear will help to repel these worms. Stalk borers also appear in mid and late summer, but you can get around this problem by planting your corn early.

The most disgusting pest of corn is a fungus, which very appropriately is called smut. Smut disfigures the ears, making them into grotesque, gray blobs. Collect smut-stricken ears as soon as you see them, and burn them to kill the smut spores.

Begin checking your corn for ripeness when the silks dry to a medium brown. Sweet corn is often ripe at this point, though field corn and some sweets are not ready until the silks turn almost black. The best way to find out if the corn is ripe is to administer the "milk" test. Puncture a kernel with your fingernail. If it bleeds clear, it's still not ready. It it spurts a milky white liquid, it's just right. If it doesn't spurt at all, you've waited too long. Refrigerate your corn after picking, if dinner is still hours away.

VARIETIES

I always feel like a kid in a candy shop when it's time to buy corn seed. There are hundreds of varieties to choose from, and most of them are great. I think it's a good idea to steer clear of the extra-earlies, though, unless you're prepared to baby them along. They're not at all drought resistant and may be described as delicate in all respects. Varieties that mature in eighty days or so are more productive and more dependable in the South.

To insure a continuous supply of fresh corn, either succession plant every three weeks or choose several varieties that mature at different rates and plant them at the same time in blocks. For example, the following group will provide six weeks worth of fresh corn when planted more or less at the same time:

Seneca Star (Yellow, takes sixty-five days)
Seneca Chief (Yellow, takes eighty-two days)
Silver Queen (White, takes ninety-four days)
Country Gentleman (White, takes one hundred days)

Miniature corn produces less food per square foot than full-sized corn, but it's fun to grow anyway. It matures rapidly and can be planted very close together. However, be prepared for a small harvest that gets eaten up quickly. One person can easily eat a half dozen ears of miniature corn at one sitting.

When choosing and evaluating corn varieties, let your taste buds be your guide. The super-sweets are, as their name implies, extremely sweet. Try them on a small scale first to see if you like that much sugar in your corn.

POPCORN should be planted and cultivated just like sweet corn. The difference comes at harvest time, when popcorn ears are left on the stalk until the shucks dry to a light brown. If the weather is wet enough to cause molds or if bugs get out of hand, shuck the mature ears and bring them indoors; then dry them in a slow one hundred-degree oven for an hour or so.

Getting the moisture content of popcorn right is no big feat — the popcorn knows. Under good conditions, popcorn may be stored on the cob, clusters of which make great Christmas presents. Or, you can remove the kernels by twisting the dry ears between your hands. Store in closed glass jars.

Make certain that you locate plantings of popcorn away from your other corn. If sweet corn is pollinated by popcorn, its sugar content will be greatly reduced.

Cucumbers

This ancient vegetable has brought crisp, cool flavor to dinner tables for thousands of years. Like air conditioning in a bowl, chilled cucumbers can help you to forget that it's ninety degrees outside — at least for awhile. Thanks to the development of the new "burpless" varieties, you also can enjoy them to your heart's content. The very best cucumbers are those which are grown in organically enriched soil, picked when still warm from the sun, and quickly chilled before slicing. They deteriorate rapidly after being picked, and thus should be refrigerated or pickled immediately after you pull them from the vine.

Cucumbers may be grown in hills, rows, or large pots, either in full sun or partial shade. Early May is the best time to plant your main crop. You also can follow up with additional plantings throughout early summer. Seeds will not germinate under scorching conditions, so start fall cucumbers indoors in July and transplant in August. Late plantings also benefit from a little dappled shade, which reduces the heat stress the plants must endure in scorching weather.

A well fed vine will produce several cucumbers. When planting in hills, work the soil at least a foot deep and spade in two heaping shovelfuls of rotted manure or compost for each hill. Before you plant the seeds, rake the hills down so that they are only two or three inches high. (If the hills are too high, they will dry out very quickly in hot weather.) When enriched with compost and protected from drought, each hill should support two plants.

A large planting of pickling cucumbers may be simpler to plant in rows. These cucumbers are picked all at once, so you don't have to be concerned about tearing up the vines as you gather the cukes. To plant, cultivate the row and make a trench down the middle eight inches deep. Place two inches of compost or manure in the bottom of the trench and refill it with soft soil. Then plant the seeds one inch deep.

Patio gardeners can enjoy fresh cucumbers, too. Choose a very large pot or tub with drainage holes in it, and fill with a planting mix that includes sandy soil and compost. Poke the seeds in about one and a half inches deep, and pat the soil to firm them in. Keep the potting mixture moist, but not overly wet, until the seedlings appear. Then water them twice a week, occasionally adding a half ration of fish emulsion to the watering can. Keep the pot in a very sunny place.

All cucumbers benefit from trellising. In fact, many of the longest, sweetest varieties must be trellised or the cukes will kink and curl. Fencing stretched between posts, three stakes drawn together at the top like a teepee, or wire cages work well as cucumber trellises. In pots, the small wire contraptions sold in stores as tomato cages are ideal cucumber supports.

Cucumbers need a rich, constant water supply. If you take a good look at a mature vine, and count all the cucumbers there, you can't help being impressed by the way the relatively skimpy plant manages such progeny. Cucumbers are more than nine-tenths water; when the roots run short of moisture, the vines have nothing to give, so the young cucumbers shrivel and new blossoms fall off. Existing fruits may turn bitter. So, in times of drought or dry heat, make sure that cucumbers get plenty of supplemental water.

Like other cucurbits, cucumbers are not shining stars in the longevity category. Disease resistant varieties, grown where they are shaded in late afternoon, stand the best chance of living a long life; but even then they also must be given supplemental waterings of manure tea. To insure a long, continuous cucumber harvest, make plantings a month apart from April to June, and once again in late July for cucumbers in the fall.

Watch cucumbers closely for evidence of insects and disease. Dust periodically with wood ashes to deter squash bugs and cucumber beetles. Bacterial wilt, a soil disease passed along by cucumber beetles, can quickly devastate a cucumber patch. Affected plants will wilt during the day and still be fully wilted the next morning. Remove them, keep your fingers crossed that the remaining plants will be safe, and don't plant cucumbers in that section of the garden again for at least two years.

Pick all cucumbers as soon as they're ripe to keep the vines from collapsing from exhaustion. The vines, stems, and leaves are very delicate, and touching them the wrong way can give them a terminal bruise. Treat your cucumbers with respect, handle them gently, and they'll pay you back with one of the best tastes of summer.

VARIETIES

Some of the new cucumber varieties are incredible. For eating fresh, try the long, burpless hybrids like *Burpless* and *Sweet Slice. Poinsett* is a widely recommended variety that's resistant to several diseases, and you can do just about anything with them. The latest thing in cucumber breeding is gynoecious hybrids, which produce all female flowers. A few seeds of normal cucumbers are included in the packet so there will be several male flowers around to supply pollen.

When planning a summer pickling project, it's worth the trouble to make separate plantings of varieties like *Tiny Dill* or *West India Gherkin* for small whole pickles, or *Liberty* for sliced pickles. Most slicing cucumbers make decent pickles, but most pickling cucumbers make inferior slicers. It pays to specialize when planning a summer's worth of cucumbers.

Eggplant

This unique vegetable is a favorite among Southerners, since it does so well in midsummer's heat. From beginning to end, eggplant is very tropical in its likes and dislikes. It craves hot weather and detests cold, and it produces best if the plants never have to go through any kind of stress except that caused by extreme heat.

Think of eggplant primarily as a crop for late summer harvest, and start seeds indoors just before the last frost, sometime in March. The young seedlings need plenty of light. If they get so big that the roots reach outside the container and you're not ready to set them out, gently move them into bigger pots. Set the plants out in late April or early May, when the soil is warm and dry. If your family eats a lot of eggplant, add a few more plants to the garden in early July.

Eggplants stay productive until frost, if they receive adequate fertilization. Place a shovelful of compost in each planting hole, and take care not to injure roots during transplanting. Water each plant with weak manure tea or fish emulsion fertilizer to help them get off to a good start. Eggplants branch out into very large plants, so place them at least two feet apart. Once they begin growing, surround them with a thick mulch of hay, leaves, or grass clippings to help hold soil moisture. If you have doubts about the fertility of your soil, place an inch of compost between the soil and the mulch.

Eggplants will produce up to a half dozen fruits at one time if you let them. You can easily manipulate eggplant production by pinching off flowers that you don't want to set fruit. If a branch already has a fruit on it that looks good, remove any other flowers that appear on that branch for a few weeks. Stop pinching blossoms from the branch when the older fruit is almost ready to cut. When handled this way, three or four plants will easily produce enough eggplants for the average household. You'll be able to gather them steadily from July through September, and perhaps beyond, depending on how long warm weather lasts.

Cut the fruits from the stem, leaving the cap attached, as soon as they reach good size and the skins have a deep, glossy color. If they become overripe, the skins lose their lustre and the fruits become bitter. Bitterness also can be caused by a shortage of water. Eggplants do not wilt when they dry out, so you have to guess when they need moisture. If it hasn't rained in a week, and daytime temperatures are in the nineties, by all means, water them.

Several insects dine on eggplant leaves, the worst of which are flea beetles. These tiny black beetles eat small holes in the leaves. Periodic applications of rotenone will control them. In hot, dry weather, spider mites also may attack your eggplants. They are very small and usually set up shop on the undersides of leaves. Unless you have a magnifying glass, the only evidence you'll see is faint, whitish netting, similar to spider webs. Blast the plants with a forceful spray of water, or spray with a mixture of water and a few drops of detergent, to get them under control. Any insects that eat tomatoes or potatoes are likely to try eggplants, too. Keep your eyes open and pick off any bugs that you catch eating leaves. Also, bear in mind that eggplants may be affected by verticillium wilt, a soil disease that primarily affects tomatoes. Avoid planting eggplants where tomatoes or potatoes were grown the year before.

VARIETIES

In our climate, it's safe to grow all varieties of eggplant, be they the dark purple bulbs most people think of when they envision this vegetable, or tapered, cylindrical fruits such as those grown in Japan. Most of the seedlings sold in garden supply centers are *Black Beauties*, a widely recommended variety that sets numerous large, bulbous fruits. *Dusky* is another bulb-shaped eggplant, and it bears a little earlier than *Black Beauty. Florida Hi Bush* also performs very well throughout the South.

In addition to these, Japanese or Chinese eggplant varieties are also good choices, but you'll probably have to start the seedlings yourself from seed. The fruits are long and slender, and not as heavy as the oval types. They can be cooked like regular eggplants or can be roasted on the grill like corn. If you really like eggplants (or if you just like to grow them to give away), you'll be impressed with the quality and productivity of these imported strains.

Garlic

Generations of garlic lovers have each made their contributions to the reputation of the most aromatic member of the onion family. You may hear that garlic wards off evil spirits, cures high blood pressure, calms the nerves, or keeps insects from biting a person who eats enough of it. I doubt that garlic is this effective in solving some of life's problems, but it certainly is an indispensable vegetable in the kitchen. Cloves of fresh, juicy garlic are not at all difficult to grow, but there are certain techniques you need to know about. The most important one is planting it at the right time.

Like many other members of the onion family, garlic is a biennial, meaning that it flowers and sets seed in its second year of life. However, producing seed is only one of the two ways garlic propagates itself. During its first year, it reproduces by division — by developing a clump of cloves under the ground. Since this is the part of the plant we eat, it's logical that the objective in growing garlic is to encourage large, vigorous one-year-old plants, which in turn will produce many large cloves.

This is where proper timing comes in. Garlic, as do other alliums, responds dramatically to long days. In late June, when days get really long, it stops whatever it's doing and goes into a state of semi-dormancy. One-year-old plants send all available energy to their roots during this time and develop fat cloves. Two-year-old plants flower. In other words, garlic "terminates" itself in one way or another in midsummer. To get a good summer crop of bulbs the first year, plant sprouting cloves in fall so they will have plenty of time to grow before they die back in summer.

Garlic is very cold-hardy, so there is little danger in planting in autumn. Freezes damage the leaves, but the underground bulbs are safely insulated from danger. Plant unpeeled cloves a foot apart, root side down, in October, but first enrich the soil with rotted manure or compost. Garlic is a moderately heavy feeder and appreciates all the help you can offer.

The cloves should promptly send up thin green shoots. Mulch around the plants with small leaves when they are a few inches tall, but allow the shoots to poke through. The plants will continue to grow slowly until the middle of winter. Then they will stop growing and wait for the cold weather to end.

New leaves begin to grow when soil temperatures rise in early spring. In March, carefully remove the mulch to help the soil warm up a little faster, and substitute a one-inch layer of rotted manure or compost. Garlic does most of its growing during the spring months, and the better it's fed during this period, the bigger the garlic bulbs will be.

When days get hot, the leaves will stop growing and gradually turn yellow. Wait until the tops turn brown and fall over before digging up the bulbs. Dig up as many as you like and let them cure in a dry place. You can eat them right away if you must, but they will keep better if they are thoroughly air dried.

Leave a few plants in the ground to use as next year's baby plants. Mark their location, for they will die back without a trace for two to three months. In the fall, the healthy bulbs will send up small shoots. At this point, you can dig them up, gently separate the young plants, and immediately replant them. Allow them a few weeks to get established, mulch lightly with small leaves, and you're back at the starting place again.

New plantings of garlic also can be made in early spring. However, since the plants have less time to grow before mid-summer casts its spell, fewer bulbs (of smaller size) should be expected. When you don't get your garlic planted until spring, I suggest skipping the summer harvest the first year. Maybe you won't have fresh garlic to eat, but you will have plenty of healthy baby plants to propagate in fall, and you'll be guaranteed a good crop of garlic *next* year.

VARIETIES

Two types of garlic are commonly grown in home gardens. One is regular *white garlic* such as you buy at the store. It is pungent and full flavored, though you'll probably discover that homegrown garlic is a little gentler than commercially produced garlic that has been in storage for awhile. The other type of garlic is often called *elephant garlic*, and many gardeners like it so well that it's all they plant. Each elephant garlic plant produces four or five huge cloves, each one four times the size of a normal garlic clove. The flavor of elephant garlic is much milder than regular garlic, and it's commonly described as a cross between garlic and onion. Use the same planting schedule with elephant garlic as with plain garlic.

I suggest that you buy your first garlic bulbs from a seed

company to be assured of good stock. However, you can plant garlic purchased from a store, provided the cloves show signs of sprouting and the root end of the bulb has not been injured or removed. Once you get started, think of your garlic as neither annual nor biennial, but as a renewable crop.

Gourds

Here's a garden plant to grow just for fun. There are gourds to use as birdhouses, gourds to make into bath sponges, and gourds that are nothing more than decoration. Gourds are a little tougher than the other cucurbits (cucumbers, squash, etc.) and stand a good chance of making it through their long growing season without being killed prematurely by insects.

Plant gourd seeds in late April or early May. They do best grown along a fence, which will support their vines and help to filter the sun a bit. The more fertilizer you give them, the more gourds you can expect, but most people don't like to use their precious manures just to grow gourds. Work in as much manure as you can spare, and mulch the young plants with newspapers or straw to keep out weeds.

Gourds can handle some abusive weather without being seriously damaged, and their thick rinds help them hold in moisture, so they are not as sensitive to drought as other cucurbits. They do, however, seem to take forever to mature. Even with our long growing season, gourds must be planted by the middle of May if they are to be big and hard by the end of September. If not fully mature when picked, they won't keep well at all.

Herbs

A small planting of kitchen herbs may be just the thing your garden needs to make it a truly great one. The flavor and aroma or freshly-picked herbs cannot be matched by the dried versions of the same plants. Generally speaking, a culinary herb is any plant grown primarily for its pungent leaves which are used as flavoring agents in food.

There are hundreds of herbs that will grow in the South, though only the true enthusiast is likely to try all of them. I suggest that you start with the ones you use most, such as parsley, basil, and chives. Add to your collection each year, and before you know it, you'll have an amazing group of plants, most of which will produce pickable leaves for several years. Since this book is about food plants, I'll stick with herbs used in cooking and discuss ten versatile ones which thrive in the South when given proper care: basil, chives, dill, mint, oregano, parsley, rosemary, sage, summer savory, and tarragon.

It's not necessary to delegate much of your garden space to growing herbs. Two good plants of any one herb should provide you with all you can use, plus plenty to give away. Herbs are not picky about where they grow, either. They like full sun and well drained soil, but beyond this, most herbs can adapt to whatever growing condition they find themselves in.

If you're just getting started with herbs, beware of a common problem. There are at least ten different kinds of oregano, almost as many types of tarragon, and countless types of parsley. Almost every major herb has a closely related cousin that is second rate as a culinary herb. If you grow a plant that doesn't look or taste like what you had in mind, get rid of it and secure new seeds or a new plant from a different source.

<u>Basil</u> is a warm weather herb that must be planted each year from seed. The seeds sprout willingly and are ready to

transplant within six weeks. Start the seeds indoors or in a cold frame in February and March, and set them out when all danger of frost is past. Leaves are ready to pick in as little as sixty days after transplanting. The most popular use for this herb is to chop and sprinkle the leaves over tomatoes and other summer vegetables.

Gather every last basil leaf before the first frost in fall. The leaves are very tender and will blacken and die overnight following a frost. Preserve basil leaves by drying them, or make them into pesto to store in the freezer. The leaves are in peak condition just before the plants flower in late summer.

Chives are a biennial and grow almost exactly like multiplying onions. You can start them from seeds or from purchased plants. Chives multiply very successfully by division, so you should have to buy them only once.

When starting chives from seed, plant them in a cold frame or on a windowsill in February. They grow slowly at first and should not be transplanted until the skinny plants have two leaves. Set them out close together, in groups.

Some harvesting may be done from first-year plants, but chives don't become really vigorous until their second year, when they also produce pretty purple flowers. Pick chives as you need them all summer, but especially early in the year before the flowers open. Dig and divide established plantings each fall. In addition to the usual onion-flavored chives, also try Chinese chives, which have a subtle garlic flavor.

Dill, like basil, is a warm weather annual that is planted from seed each spring. The feathery plants are large and lacy in appearance, so you might consider planting dill in your flower garden, too. Both the leaves and seeds are edible and can be used to flavor pickles, breads, salads, and many other dishes.

Dill does not transplant well, so it's best to sow the seeds directly in prepared garden soil. They should sprout in one to two weeks. Thin the plants to at least six inches apart and mulch with hay to retain soil moisture and prevent weeds. Dill leaves should be harvested before the plants flower. Don't pick too much foliage from plants being grown primarily for seeds.

Mints grow so vigorously that steps must be taken to keep them in check. They produce many seeds, but the most effective way they reproduce is by sending out lateral roots, which establish themselves as individual plants the same way bermuda grass and blackberries do. You can stop mint from spreading by installing a piece of tin around the bed or by digging out the new plants as they pop up.

There are many mint variations, including peppermint, spearmint, orange mint, pineapple mint, and others. Unless you know of a source for cuttings, the only way to get rare varieties is to start them from seeds. Mints sprout within a month, when planted in a cold frame or on a windowsill in February. Cuttings root so fast that they may be planted directly in the garden, provided that at least three inches of the stem is buried beneath good soil.

Gather mint leaves to be dried and used as tea herbs in early July, before the plants start to flower. Mint leaves can be gathered at all other times of the year, though they get pretty raggedy when the plants are in full flower. If you cut your mint back to a height of ten inches after the flowers fade, new growth will quickly appear. In mild years, a few mint leaves will remain pickable throughout the winter.

Oregano is a true delight once you get it started. Unfortunately, the best oreganos are also the poorest sprouters, so I suggest buying starter plants. Or, you can become friends with someone who has a good oregano plant and talk them into giving you a four-inch cutting of a growing tip. Plant the cutting in vermiculite and keep it in a sunny windowsill. Oregano tolerates cold pretty well and usually will winter over under a thick mulch. If you don't want to take chances, dig up part of a plant in September and replant it in a pot. This way, you'll have fresh leaves all winter, plus a vigorous plant to set out in the spring.

Parsley is a cold-natured biennial which will produce pickable leaves year-round if you remember to start new plants at least once a year. For top production, start two new plants in February and two more in September. The seeds are slow germinators and often take up to three weeks to sprout. Use only fresh seeds, and soak them overnight before planting. Spring-planted parsley does well in a cold frame.

Transplant parsley seedlings very carefully, disturbing the root system as little as possible. Water regularly until the plants begin to grow. Harvest from each plant a few leaves at a time. Parsley loves cool weather and produces heavy yields until it flowers.

Parsley variations include *Italian flat* parsley, the extra curly *Green Moss* variety, and numerous ones in between. *Paramount* and *Evergreen* are excellent varieties for the home garden.

Rosemary is almost impossible to grow from seed. The germination rate is low and the seeds which do sprout take several weeks to start growing. It's much easier to take a cutting and root it in vermiculite, and easier yet to buy a starter plant.

Set out rosemary late in the spring. Place it somewhere that's convenient to water, for it cannot tolerate drought. Pick leaves freely in early summer, but baby the plants through summer dry spells. Sometimes rosemary will winter over in the garden, but that's a risky proposition. In September, dig up part of a plant, set it in a pot, and bring it indoors before hard freezes commence. Replant potted rosemary in early April, and propagate a new plant from stem cuttings when new growth appears.

Sage is an incredibly productive herb which sprouts readily from seed sown indoors, or in a cold frame, in early spring. By the end of June, there are plenty of individual leaves to pick, but they don't develop their fullest flavor until the hot days of August. Stem cuttings also root easily if taken after the plants reach full size.

Sage is very winter-hardy and comes back every year. However, the plants become rather woody after two years, and it's best to start new ones at that time. Be careful when cooking with fresh sage, for its flavor is very strong. Dry extra leaves whole and crush them as you use them. Two sage plants produce enough leaves to supply several households for a year.

Summer savory has a delicate flavor that goes perfectly with beans and other summer vegetables. Since it is a fast-growing annual, you can scatter the seeds in the bean patch at planting time. They germinate in about two weeks. The plants themselves are often straggly and benefit from frequent pinching back. Heavy harvesting also delays flowering a little. After flowering, summer savory dies and you have to replant it.

This herb also grows well in pots or hanging baskets. However, pots limit root size, and it's important to fertilize pot-grown savory once a month, preferably with a weak solution of fish emulsion fertilizer.

Don't confuse summer savory with winter savory, which has a much sharper flavor. Winter savory is a nice addition to the herb garden, but most folks prefer the milder flavor of summer savory for cooking.

Tarragon is a must, if you enjoy French cuisine. It's a hardy perennial that grows into a tall, bushy plant each summer. Real French tarragon does not produce viable seeds, but is propagated by digging and dividing the plants in early spring. Tarragon leaves lose much of their flavor when dried, and tarragon vinegar is the preferred method for keeping them. Use the flavored vinegar in salads, or fish out the tarragon leaves and chop them into sauces, butters, or poultry dishes.

When buying tarragon plants, beware of Russian tarragon, which is only remotely similar to French or German tarragon. Although it grows vigorously and produces viable seeds, the Russian version has inferior flavor. Only French tarragon has the smooth, delicate flavor needed for accenting your favorite dishes.

Jerusalem Artichoke

This root vegetable is in no way related to globe artichokes. It's actually a member of the daisy family and is a botanical cousin to the sunflower. A native plant of North America, Jerusalem artichokes thrive in any garden soil and are a cinch to grow. The edible part of the plant is the root, which is eaten like a boiled potato. Its flavor is rather sweet yet contains no starch. The sugar in Jerusalem artichokes is insulin, which is safe for consumption by diabetics.

Plant this unusual vegetable in mid-spring, after potatoes but before beans. No supplemental fertilizer is needed if the soil is of reasonably good quality. Jerusalem artichokes stay in the ground all summer and grow very tall. Place seeds or small tubers a foot apart. When the plants are a foot tall, mulch with grass clippings or hay. Once this is done, you can safely neglect your Jerusalem artichokes until it's time to dig them up in fall. They usually shade out most of the weeds that germinate in surrounding soil, especially if they have been mulched. They also may shade out neighboring plants, so place them along the edge of the garden or next to a crop such as bush beans that can stand a little shade.

Some people even lop off the tops of the plants in mid-season to keep them from growing so tall that they cast huge shadows on other garden vegetables. To do this, simply cut off the main stem at a point about four feet from the ground. This one-time pruning does not reduce production, provided the plants are healthy and vigorous when you do it.

Carefully dig up every plant in late fall, just before the first killing frost. Watch for small stray tubers and pick them up, even if they're not big enough to eat. If left in the soil, these will grow into huge plants in spring. It's fine to go ahead and preplant them right away, for small tubers winter over well if covered with two inches of soil and a little mulch. Just be sure to move them from year to year, and expect a few strays to pop up here and there in the garden. They're pretty easy to dig out, but it's simpler to control their propagation by allowing small roots to grow only in assigned places.

Jerusalem artichokes planted at the same time will be of uniform size, but the size of the mature tubers is highly variable. The largest ones are the easiest ones to eat, and you may opt to dispose of any excess supply of tiny ones. Scrub freshly dug roots and then steam or boil them whole. Peel, when they're cool enough to handle, and cut into bite-sized pieces. Sprinkle with lemon juice and a litle melted butter for an unusual, nutty tasting treat.

Kale

Every person I know who has ever grown kale has adopted it as a leading vegetable in their fall garden. Certainly one reason for this is that kale produces an abundant harvest in the middle of winter, long after other garden vegetables are dead and gone. Kale is also a choice crop because of its sweet flavor and crispy texture — not at all what you'd expect from a plant that looks like frilly collards. Kale doesn't taste much like collards at all, and is good to eat either raw or cooked.

Kale is very easy to grow, as long as you plant it at the right time. Sow seeds in a well cultivated bed in late August, and choose a place where other brassicas (cabbage, broccoli, etc.) were not grown recently. Enrich the bed with an inch of com-

101

post and some wood ashes — kale does not like extremely acidic soil. The weather is unkind to germinating seeds in late summer, so sow the seeds thickly and expect a germination rate in the fifty percent range. You may need to water every few days to get the seeds up.

The seedlings should begin to grow vigorously when they are about a month old. Kale thrives in cool weather, and light frost does not slow it down. The most productive plants are those which have just reached full size when hard freezes begin. Start gathering hand-sized leaves *after* the plants have been through several frosts, for freezing temperatures trigger sugar production in the leaves. Kale that's picked when the weather is still warm will be of inferior quality and may taste slightly bitter.

As winter progresses, you should expect your kale to be damaged from time to time by hard freezes. Don't worry. The plants will survive and will even grow new leaves in between cold snaps. Kale faces up to winter courageously and can be picked continuously until the middle of February. But as soon as spring days warm up, existing leaves lose their fair flavor and no new leaves appear. Instead, the plants send up tall branches of pretty yellow flowers.

It's fine to allow your kale to set seed if you can spare the space. The seeds won't be ripe until the beginning of August, but when the pods finally dry and split, you'll have all the kale seeds you can use — just in time for planting. Besides producing good seeds, kale which is allowed to stand in the garden produces a light second crop of leaves, which are suitable for cooking. After the seedpods have filled, small bunches of new leaves sprout from the main stem, just below the seed-bearing branches. While they are not as sweet as kale harvested in winter, these summer leaves are surprisingly mild, and I think they are as good as any other cooking green grown in summer.

VARIETIES

Dwarf Blue Curled Scotch Vates is an excellent strain, as is *Dwarf Green Curled*, which is very similar. *Dwarf Siberian* and other Siberian varieties are not as sweet as these, but they are more tolerant of extreme cold. That's one characteristic we

Southerners don't really need, so I suggest growing only the better tasting Vates relatives.

Lettuce

The notion that crisp heads of lettuce can't be grown in the South is a myth. In reality, mild, crunchy heads of lettuce are one of the simplest crops to coax from your garden soil. All this vegetable needs to make it happy is cool weather, plenty of water, and someone to pick it when it reaches peak condition.

The cool weather requirement hangs up some people who haven't caught on to using late winter and fall as active growing seasons. Lettuce should be one of the first crops planted in early spring and also should be a major crop in the fall. In between, in the heat of summer, the best you can hope for is some loose leaf, not-so-crisp specimens to eat on tomato sandwiches.

Begin planting lettuce in late winter, as soon as the soil can be worked. Or, better yet, prepare planting beds in fall so they'll be ready to plant in February without having to cultivate them first. When preparing the soil, work in a little compost or manure, but not too much. Lettuce roots are skimpy and don't need much food. Later, when the plants are half grown, top dressing with compost, manure, and a good mulch will take care of possible nutritional shortages.

You can get an early start by planting seeds in cloche-covered beds. In early February, scatter some seeds on a pre-pared bed and cover them with one-fourth to one-half inch of fine soil. Then place a cloche over the bed, and keep the soil moist until the seedlings emerge. When the weather warms and hard freezes end, remove the cloche and thin the seedlings so they do not touch one another. The thinnings are fine to eat, or you can move them to other parts of the garden. Lettuces will not head when crowded. If big heads are what you want, it's better to thin too much than too little.

In mid-March, make another sowing of lettuce, followed by a third planting in early April. This staggered planting schedule will produce a long, slow harvest throughout the spring lettuce season. Lettuce plants of the same variety planted at the same time mature all at once. Since it must be eaten fresh (and not all at once), it's best to plant only a little at a time. A good rule of thumb is to limit plantings to one square yard each, unless you have a very large family.

Lettuce bolts when the days become long and hot, and there is nothing you can do to stop it. As soon as the plants switch gears and enter their reproductive phase (bolting), the leaves become bitter; you might as well pull them up and add them to the compost heap. If your heading lettuce does not "head up," you're either planting too late or not thinning enough.

Slugs and snails can pose problems for lettuce, especially in years when spring weather is very wet. Prevent damage by keeping lettuce thinned and relatively free of weeds so air can circulate freely around the plants. Saucers of beer set out among the lettuce in the evening are effective traps for slugs, who like beer better than lettuce. Rabbits like tender spring lettuce better than just about anything, so you'll need to either fence off the area, keep the bed covered with a wire cloche, or lay down a "scent" fence of used cat litter around the edge to keep them away.

In May, just before the weather gets really hot, make a small planting of loose leaf lettuce. Non-heading lettuces tolerate heat and drought pretty well and help to extend the salad season until the first tomatoes ripen. Choose a spot that gets a few hours of shade each day — too much sun can make even loose leaf lettuce taste bitter. Begin picking the lettuce leaves as soon as they begin to bunch. It's safe to gather up to half of the leaves present in each picking, for the plants quickly will produce new leaves, especially after a soaking rain.

The same lettuce varieties that you grow in spring may be planted again in late summer for fall harvest. However, they need cool temperatures for germination, and the first fall planting cannot be seeded directly in hot garden soil. Instead, start seeds indoors in a sunny windowsill or outdoors in a shady place. After the seedlings emerge, make sure they get plenty of sunshine and water until they're big enough to handle. Wait for a spell of mild weather and carefully set them out in the garden, placing a handful of compost under each one. Then keep them watered until they become adjusted, and water regularly if rain is scarce. Mulches are especially beneficial to fall lettuce, since they help keep the soil cool and moist. Start fall seeds around the first of August, set them out in early September, and enjoy the harvest until a killer freeze comes along. Since late fall days are short and cool, mature lettuce will "wait" to be picked for a long time, so it's safe to plant the whole crop more or less at once. Fast-maturing varieties may be planted directly in the garden in early September. If a hard freeze threatens late plantings before they're ready to pick, cover them with a cloche.

VARIETIES

There are dozens of varieties of lettuce which perform well in our region. I recommend trying every variety that sounds good to you, and growing at least one new variety every year. Under good conditions, lettuce seeds will keep for three years or longer, so it's practical to buy several seed packets and take two or three years to use them up. I plant at least three varieties each year and would plant more if I thought someone would eat it all.

The main reason to plant different varieties of lettuce is that eating the same combination salad day after day gets monotonous. Certainly all salads taste good, but part of a salad's overall appeal is its looks. Your family is less likely to experience salad burn-out during lettuce season if you vary the ingredients from one salad to the next by using different kinds of lettuce. Generally speaking, lettuces can be lumped into four categories: crisp head, butterhead, loose leaf, and cos or romaine.

In the crisp head group, large green leaves surround a

tight, light green head. These varieties must be planted quite early, and they can take up to ten weeks to mature. I particularly like *Mission*, which is darker green than most heading varieties, and *Great Lakes*, a dependable variety for crisp, sweet heads.

Butterhead varieties have loose heads surrounded by dark green leaves which have thick, crisp ribs. They are very dependable and fast to mature. My all-time lettuce favorites, *Augusta* and *Buttercrunch*, are butterheads.

Loose leaf varieties form little or no head and are not as crisp as heading types. However, they tolerate heat better, so you can plant them relatively late in the spring. Pale green *Salad Bowl* and red colored *Ruby* are both frilly and beautiful. *Oak Leaf* is the most heat-tolerant lettuce variety that I know of.

Cos or romaine varieties include *Paris, Valmaine*, and *Barcarolle*. They take longer to mature than most other lettuces and must be planted very early in spring. They don't exactly form heads, but have mild, crunchy, inner leaves that are blanched by large outer leaves. If your favorite salad is Caesar, you'll want to experiment with these European varieties.

Melons

It would be hard to find a person who doesn't enjoy biting into a sweet, juicy melon. They're not the easiest garden crop to grow, but melons deserve a place in every backyard garden — if only for the delicious, sensuous pleasure they bring to the table.

There are so many kinds of melons that it might take a lifetime of gardening to give each of them a trial in your own garden. Each year seedsmen introduce melons from various corners of the world, and some of these are splendid. Also, old standbys like cantaloupes (which northerners call musk-melons) constantly are being improved through selective breeding. But many of the most luscious melon varieties never will be available in grocery stores, because their thin skins and juicy flesh are so delicate that they can't be shipped. In the backyard garden, however, they can be a great success.

No matter what types of melons you decide to grow (cantaloupes, honeydews, Japanese melons, watermelons, etc.), you'll have to make your own luck, for melons have some peculiar cultural requirements. They also suffer the same insect pests as other cucurbits, so it's doubly important that the plants be as healthy and vigorous as possible.

Melons grow only in warm weather and do best if they can grow for a few weeks in spring before the days get too hot. For best results, plant them in late April or May. Watermelons tolerate heat better than other melons and can be planted a little later, thus stretching the harvest. Most melons mature all at once, so stagger planting dates if several varieties with similar maturation times are to be grown.

The following planting instructions may sound compli-cated, but they make sense when you consider a melon's quirky root system. Along with a network of tender roots that grows beneath the soil surface, melons also send down feeder roots that may reach as deep as ten feet. The result is a jellyfish-like root structure unlike any other vegetable in the garden. Be-cause of this, good melons require special planting.

RESERVOIR PLANTING

The objective at planting time is to provide a full season's supply of nutrients for both the shallow roots and the deep ones. One way to do this would be to dig a deep, deep hole under the planting site, which loosens the soil and makes it easier for the roots to "feed." But this is impractical — you'd have to dig all day to plant one hill of melons. Therefore, many gardeners have adopted another way of planting melons that serves the plants' needs without taking up the whole weekend. I call it reservoir planting.

The idea is to supply a place where the deep roots can

RESERVOIR PLANTING MELONS

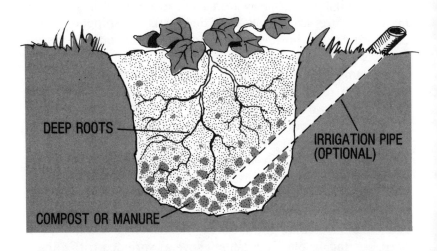

DEEP ROOTS

IRRIGATION PIPE
(OPTIONAL)

COMPOST OR MANURE

effectively gather nutrients regardless of weather conditions. Since many nutrients are water soluble, and water movement in deep soil is slow, the underground reservoir serves as an oasis for deep feeder roots. To make such a reservoir, "plant" a nutrient-rich mattress a couple of *feet* beneath the planting site where the deep roots eventually will find it. Following are some ideal materials to use for this purpose (amounts needed per threesome of plants):

—four heaping shovelfuls of compost (can be slightly rough)

—three shovelfuls of horse or cow manure, chopped into two shovelfuls of garden soil

—three shovelfuls of corncobs (the more rotten, the better) mixed with two shovelfuls of compost or rotten manure.

In an ideal year for melons (one in which a heavy rain comes just after the vines have set fruit and moderate rains fall once or twice a week thereafter), simply laying in a fertilizer reservoir probably will meet the nutritional needs of melons. But few years are so kind. Rain typically tapers off in midsummer, a few weeks before the melons are ripe. It often becomes necessary to irrigate the reservoir in order to help the deep roots reach the stockpile buried beneath. There are several ways to do this.

The simplest way is to deep water the plants, either by drip irrigation or by watering them several times in one day. However, you can save water by pounding a length of pipe into the soil that reaches right into the reservoir. The pipe (any pipe at least one inch wide) may be laid in when the seeds are planted, or you can carefully tap them in when watering season begins. Lay these irrigation pipes in at an angle, rather than straight up and down, and they will hold more water and be a little easier to remove at the end of the season.

If you have a plot of struggling melons that were planted without a reservoir, you still can invigorate them by piping manure tea or fish emulsion fertilizer down to the deep roots, or by giving the plants a thorough deep watering with one of these liquid fertilizers.

The planting method I've described involves planting melon seeds in hills. To obtain the look of row planting, arrange the hills in a line, leaving six feet between hills. When the vines run, they will cover the space between hills. If the vines go crazy and invade the rest of the garden, *gently* move the offending vines to where you want them. Some varieties cannot take even the most lighthanded touch, evidenced by wilting leaves the day after the vine is moved. When such damage occurs, cleanly pinch off the damaged vine.

MULCHING MELONS

Shade from the foliage that runs along the ground is nature's way of keeping the shallow roots of melon vines protected in hot weather. In our climate, however, this is not enough, for the top few inches of soil can easily dry out in a few days. Consequently, it is important to mulch your melons.

Unfortunately, most organic mulches are dangerous to use with melons, since they provide a place for squash bugs and cucumber beetles to hide. Black plastic, newspapers, or a shallow layer of sawdust are better choices. If you decide not to mulch your melons (not an altogether bad idea), lay a piece of folded newspaper under each fruit as it grows to protect the rind from insects and rot.

Cucumber beetles and squash bugs are likely to go after honeydews, cantaloupes, and Japanese melons. To control squash bugs, spray the plants thoroughly with water, wait a few minutes, and handpick the bugs. Cucumber beetles are more formidable, and it's not realistic to try to eliminate all of them. However, dusting plants periodically with rock phosphate dust, wood ashes, or rotenone will keep them at a manageable level.

Melons planted in midsummer for fall harvest mature slowly, since the days are so short. To keep them moving along, pinch off new flowers and infant melons in August. This helps the vines to channel more energy to fruits that will have time to mature before frost. Melons cannot tolerate frost.

WONDERFUL WATERMELONS

After reading these troublesome directions for growing melons, you may be ready to forget the whole thing and keep on buying stale melons at the supermarket. But don't get discouraged too fast, because watermelons are an exception to all these rules. Insects that decimate tender melons skip right over watermelons, and the hard rinds hold plenty of water. They're happy running over any kind of mulch — hay, shredded bark, or whatever you have. To put it simply, watermelons grow beautifully with very little care and infrequent supplemental watering.

Still, it's a good idea to provide a manure reservoir underneath watermelon hills. Also, when growing the seedless hybrids, be sure to plant a seeded pollinator nearby, or you'll end up with plenty of blossoms and few, if any, melons. Suggested pollinators are listed on the seed packets.

The last tip I have for growing any kind of melons is to pick them when they're fully ripe. Different types of melons, however, show ripeness in different ways. Cantaloupes and honeydews become soft at the blossom end as they ripen. When fully ripe, their stems separate from the fruit so that you can pick them with a very gentle tug. They also start to smell like a melon when ripe. Some of the new French imports should be cut before they are fully ripe and allowed to sit at room temperature, like pears, for several days before eating. However, most melons are like their botanic cousins, the berries, and should be allowed to ripen on the vine.

Watermelons do not soften as they ripen, but the stem and the curlicue become dry and lose their color as the perfect harvest day approaches. When you thump a ripe watermelon with your finger, the sound should be deep and full, since the melon is pumped full of water. In rural areas, blackbirds and crows check watermelons daily by thumping them with their beaks. When they have almost pecked a hole in the rind, harvest the melon.

VARIETIES

The most desirable melons you can grow are the honeydews. Expect to pick one to two melons per plant, depending on variety. *Earlidew* and *Venus* are dependable hybirds which slip from the vine when fully ripe. A new type of melon, which is more like a Crenshaw than a honeydew, is called *Honeyshaw*; it has creamy light orange flesh, is very large, and is certain to please any melon lover.

There are numerous good varieties of orange-fleshed cantaloupe, which withstand heat and resist insect attacks a little better than honeydews. *Alaska, Chaca*, and *Saticoy* resist some diseases and usually bear two good melons per plant.

Among the small Japanese melons, I recommend *Golden Crispy* and *Sakata's Sweet*. These melons grow almost like cucumbers, and you may want to trellis them to save space.

When it comes to watermelons, you may want to steer clear of the largest varieties, unless you have a large field in which to grow them. At harvest time, you'll also appreciate watermelons that are small enough to fit in your refrigerator. *Sugar Baby* has a strong reputation as the best tasting of the small watermelons. *Kengarden* is a small bush-type watermelon that's easy to grow in the home garden. Yellow-fleshed watermelons like *Golden Midget* and *Yellow Baby* are an interesting change of pace, and they're no more difficult to grow than red watermelons.

Mustard

This leafy green, originally from Asia, has become a popular garden crop among Southerners because it's so easy to grow. Mustard will flourish in any soil and can withstand changes in the weather better than other greens. The leaves have a spicier flavor than either turnips or collards and contain as many vitamins as spinach. However, if you don't like cooked greens, don't bother to plant this crop. Raw mustard greens are practically inedible.

Mustard greens may be planted in early spring and again in early fall, although they tend to do a little better in the fall. These fast-growing greens require little fertilization. Plant the seeds about one-quarter inch deep and water them in. The seeds sprout vigorously, and small leaves usually are ready to pick about a month after planting. Mustard plants grow very large, so you'll probably want to plant only a few square feet of them at a time.

Mustard greens grown in cool weather are much milder than those subjected to heat, so harvest spring crops at the earliest possible time. However, mustard that matures in cool, fall weather keeps its flavor a long time. If you pick only a few leaves from each plant at a time, one sowing made in early fall will produce until hard freezes finally kill the plants. In autumn, many gardeners make mixed plantings of mustard and turnips. The two vegetables make a very flavorful mess of greens when cooked together.

VARIETIES

Two varieties of mustard, *Southern Giant Curled* and *Florida Broadleaf*, are widely available. Some people avoid curled types, since the leaves tend to hold dirt and thus are harder to clean. A new type of mustard, *Tendergreen*, often is referred to as a cross between spinach and mustard. The leaves are relatively flat, with a thick texture and full-bodied flavor.

 # Okra

For Southerners, growing okra is a snap. The weather does most of the work, for just about all okra needs to produce well is a three-month span of hot, humid weather. The planting instructions might as well be "throw some seeds in the ground and watch them grow."

Okra, originally from Africa, demands warm soil and should be planted later than many crops — in mid-May or early June. If planted while the soil is still cool, the seeds probably will germinate, but the plants won't grow until hot weather comes. To keep the seedlings from being unnecessarily ravaged by spring rains, wait until the weather settles to plant okra. A second sowing in late June or early July will insure a continuous harvest until the first frost.

Only a little fertilization is needed for this crop. An inch of manure or compost worked into the soil at planting time is sufficient, especially if the row is later mulched with grass clippings, hay, or some other organic material. Plant seeds one inch deep and about five inches apart. When they have three leaves, thin to twelve inches apart. Planting in rows makes harvesting easier, but okra also may be planted in hills or beds.

113

Just be sure that it's planted so that you can easily reach each plant when the time comes to collect the pods.

Okra pods should be cut when they're two to four inches long. If allowed to get much bigger, the pods will be tough and stringy. Use a sharp knife, kitchen scissors, or a hand-sized pruning shears to gather your okra, and cut at least twice a week. If you cut only when the plants are dry and wear a long-sleeved shirt, the prickly spines won't get under your skin and drive you crazy with itching. At the beginning of September, cut off the central stem of each plant to encourage branching. Late cuttings can then be taken from the side shoots.

Okra usually makes it through the long growing season with no problems from insects, although aphids sometimes colonize the stalks. If the infestation becomes severe, spray the plants with a mixture of water, a squirt of liquid detergent, and a few drops of peppermint oil.

A more serious problem with okra is nematodes — worm-like organisms which inhabit the soil and attack plant roots. Never plant okra in soil you know to be infested with nematodes.

VARIETIES

Clemson Spineless is the most popular variety of okra, but there are others worth trying, too. If you're super-susceptible to itching from okra spines, try *Lee* or another dwarf variety. Only the plants are dwarf (not the pods), and because of their short stature, they're easier to harvest from. Red okra is also worth trying at least once. The pods turn green when cooked.

Onions

If you have in mind growing bushels of hard, pungent storage onions to enjoy on dreary January nights, you'll have to move farther north. In the South, even if you manage to harvest a crop of keeping-quality onions, the humidity inevitably will get them once they're in storage. But this doesn't mean that you should forget about growing onions, only that you should think about it more carefully.

There are many different kinds of onions, but for the purpose of discussion, I've divided them into seven categories: (1) Bulb onions grown from seeds or seedlings (2) Bulb onions grown from sets (3) Green onions or scallions grown from seed (4) Leeks (5) Shallots (6) Egyptian multiplying onions, and (7) Bunching, multiplying onions. Each type of onion is grown a little differently and is harvested at a different time, but they all have some shared characteristics. For example, all onions have scant root systems which hang very close to the plants. Onions, therefore, are limited in how far they can reach to gather nutrients. They are further handicapped because their leaf surface (and photosynthetic ability) is limited by the shape of their leaves, so it's important to furnish them with plenty of diverse plant nutrients — nitrogen, phosphorous, potassium, manganese, copper, and even boron. You can't get this kind of broad spectrum fertilization using simple chemical fertilizers. Onions, perhaps more than any other garden crop, need the array of nutrients found in rotten manure and compost. They also need plenty of water, but not so much that they drown or that the nutrients in the soil are washed away.

BULB ONIONS FROM SEEDS

For the biggest and best crop of onion bulbs, I recommend starting your own plants from seeds. Home-grown seedlings give you the opportunity to experiment with onions of varying color, shape, and flavor. Just be sure to use fresh, well-kept seeds and to keep track of your onion-growing ventures by making notes.

Start onion seeds indoors in late winter for transplanting to the garden in February and March, or start them in late September for setting out in November. Onions need an excellent planting medium and constant moisture, so you'll get better germination by starting the seeds indoors. Direct-seeding outdoors requires a soft, peaty bed, daily sprinklings, and a patient nature.

When the grassy seedlings have two leaves, take a pair of scissors and trim them to a uniform four-inch height, and follow up with a dose of weak fish emulsion fertilizer. If weather permits, set the flats outdoors for a week or two to toughen them up. Meanwhile, prepare a rich, well drained bed. Gently place the seedlings three inches apart in the bed, being careful not to bruise the roots and neck of each plant. When setting the seedlings in fall, space them two inches apart, for some won't make it through the winter.

Give the plants a couple of weeks to get established and then start weeding. Even if you're short of time, give the bed a thorough hand weeding when the plants have three nice leaves. This is one garden chore where you'll either have to wear a glove or get your fingernails dirty, for weeding with hoes and other large tools can damage roots. Once the weeds are out, mulch one-half inch of sawdust or one inch of grass clippings. This will help to hold moisture in the soil and give the bulbs something soft to press against when they begin to swell.

By the end of April, the plants should be growing vigorously. The bigger they get at this point, the bigger the bulbs will be. If rain is scarce, water them thoroughly once a week. Bulbs will begin forming in late June as the days get long. The bulbs will have almost reached full size when the tops fall over. Dig carefully a week to ten days after the tops fall.

When harvesting onion bulbs, remove only the big clods of dirt and leave as many of the dry scales intact as possible — they contain an enzyme which inhibits sprouting. Let the whole onion plants dry in a warm, ventilated place for two weeks before bringing them indoors. Pick out any that produced flower heads and use them first. Trim the tops from the others, place them in mesh bags, and use as needed. Onions seldom keep for more than three months in our climate. Chop up the extra ones before they go bad and freeze them.

BULB ONIONS FROM SETS

Onion sets are very easy to find, and they're a dependable way to grow onion bulbs. As with growing onions from seeds, it's important to get them up and growing as early as possible. Sets usually are planted in early spring, but they also may be stuck in the ground in late fall. Like seedling onions, they need good, fertile soil.

The most crucial aspect of growing onions from sets is choosing the right size. The best size sets for growing big bulbs are those about the diameter of a dime. Larger ones are likely to develop flower stalks, and smaller ones may not survive. I usually plant the little ones, but only after I've planted the oversized ones together in a separate place. These rapidly grow into fine green onions, which are ready to pull in only a few weeks. They don't need much fertilizer if they're being harvested as scallions, for most of what they need is already being stored in the big set.

Dime-sized sets have just enough stored nutrients to get them off to a fast start. Roots appear within days after planting, often before the tops. This fast start sells many gardeners on growing onions from sets. Once they're going, they need the same care as seedling onions — regular weeding, water, and plenty of sunshine. Unless you're unusually lucky, some of the onions will produce seedheads. Eat the small bulbs from these plants as soon as possible, for they will not store well.

The varieties which most sets include are on the pungent side. Some onion hobbyists are able to grow their own sets from new varieties that mature when days are shorter than fifteen hours — the amount of sunlight that normally triggers the bulbing process. Because our area gets fourteen hours of sunlight at most, growing sets is hit or miss. Most often, you end up with oversized seedlings that aren't good for much. If you're determined to give home-grown sets a shot, start seeds in a prepared bed in April and thin to no more than one inch apart. Harvest the tiny bulbs when the tops fall, and dry them just like miniature bulb onions. You may need to re-dry them periodically, if they're held until spring before being planted.

GREEN ONIONS FROM SEED

Young onions of any kind may be pulled and used as scallions, but a few onion varieties outshine the others when it comes to the quality of the green onions they produce. Specialized varieties such as *Evergreen White Bunching* are more tender than regular onions and stay that way for a long time — sometimes through the winter. If you love scallions, it's simple to grow two good crops a year — spring and fall.

As with other onion seeds, the germination rate is better if the seeds are started indoors. However, I can't justify spending the time involved in transplanting for a cheap and simple vegetable like this. So I dump a whole packet of seed in a prepared garden bed around Labor Day, and if I'm lucky with the weather, about half of them come up. (Spring plantings made this way usually wash away or rot in place). Scallions rarely need thinning. If there are too many, extras may be interplanted in small groups with other vegetables. Hill a little extra soil or mulch around the plants about a week before pulling them to help blanch the stems, thus making the tender, white part a little longer and a little more tender. Scallions usually grow slowly, so don't worry if it takes them a while to get going.

LEEKS

Leeks inspire me. Once they're up, I've never had one to die. They are dependable, easy to grow, and a delicious gourmet treat. They're also ready to harvest between green onions and bulbing onions in the spring, and after most other vegetables are gone in the fall.

Leeks are long-season annuals. They may be started from seeds in September and set out in the garden in November, or you can plant them indoors in late winter and set them out in early spring. The seedlings are very cooperative about waiting in their cups or flats until the weather is right for planting. They grow best in cool weather and are very cold-hardy. To get really big leeks, start them in the fall and let them winter over in the garden, surrounded by a modest mulch.

Trench planting often is recommended for leeks, that is, seedlings are planted in the bottom of a four-inch deep trough. At first, only enough soil is added to securely anchor the roots, but as the plants mature, more soil is added until the trench is completely filled. You'll get good, long leeks this way, but they'll be loaded with grit. I'd rather let the leeks be a little shorter but clean, and so I don't plant in trenches. Instead, I plant the seedlings about one and a half inches deep and leave them alone until they're about a foot tall. Then I mulch them generously with straw, which does a good job of blanching the stems.

Harvest leeks when they are three-fourths to one and a half inches in diameter but before seedheads appear. You'll need to dig them out with a shovel, for they have many strong roots. Extra leeks are a cinch to dry, but they must be cleaned first to remove dirt trapped between the layers. To clean, cut off the top few inches of leaves and all of the roots except the nub. Cut a slit down one side from the top to within one inch of the base. Open the leek with your fingers and rinse it out under cold, running water.

SHALLOTS

The main reason to grow shallots is that they don't taste like any other onion. Mild yet flavorful, shallots are considered a gourmet vegetable. They are not very productive, however, and you simply don't get much food from each plant. But they're simple enough to grow and very good for interplanting with other vegetables in spring.

Start with sets rather than seeds, and set them out very early in the spring. Don't plant them too deeply — shallots do best in soft soil, growing just below the soil line. Space them four inches apart, keep them weeded, and harvest in midsummer when the tops die back.

After harvest, allow the bulbs to dry for a few weeks and then store them in the refrigerator. Select the very best bulbs for next year's crop and keep them in a cool, dry place. If you don't think these "keepers" will stay in good condition until next spring planting time, go ahead and plant them in mid-fall and let them winter over.

MULTIPLYING ONIONS

It's probably improper to speak of multiplying onions as perennials, for the same plants do not come back year after year. However, multipliers reproduce enthusiastically by division, and once you get a crew of them growing, you'll never have to buy starter plants again. Multipliers are common throughout the South, and no old-time garden was complete without them. While they're a fine addition to any garden, they're particularly handy to have right outside the back door — even if that means they must grow in partial shade. The closer they are to the cutting board, the more you'll come to depend on them in the kitchen.

EGYPTIAN MULTIPLIERS

Egyptian multipliers are the sexiest member of the onion family. They're increasingly popular, and the old way of obtaining them (as a gift from a gardening friend) is quickly being replaced by their commercial availability. What distinguishes Egyptians from other multipliers is the way they reproduce. A flower head shoots out of each plant in midsummer, but instead of developing seeds, baby onions start growing right there on the tops of the plants. Sometimes even the babies will have babies before the mother stalk bends over so that the new plants can take root. It's a strange and interesting process to watch, but it does interrupt the harvest. Egyptians are best harvested in early spring, for they quickly toughen up in preparation for their flamboyant procreation. However, if the babies are planted in early summer, they can be used as scallions in the fall.

Planting the babies (bulblets) is only one of two ways to propagate Egyptians. They also may be dug and divided in spring or fall. The onions fare better if mature bulblet clusters are planted in one piece, given some time to develop roots, and then divided and replanted. For foolproof results, plant whole bulblet clusters in June so that the root nub is barely covered with soil. As soon as they green up in October, dig them up, break apart, and re-plant.

BUNCHING ONIONS

Smaller and more delicate than Egyptians, bunching multipliers grow primarily by division. Some are known as Japanese onions, and I've also heard them called clone onions. They are slender and grow in tight bunches, appearing early in the spring, dying back in midsummer, and reappearing again in the fall.

What makes bunching onions so desirable is that they stay in pickable condition for a long time. To harvest, I dig up a bunch, pull off as many as I'll need for a few days, and replant the leftovers in clumpettes of three or four onions. They do better if not planted as singles. To keep your bunching onions productive, dig and divide them in either early spring or fall.

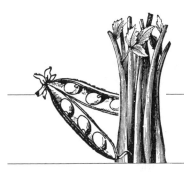

Oriental Vegetables

In our melting pot culture, vegetables which start out as European, African, South American, or Asian don't stay that way very long. Our climate has proved highly adaptable to plants from around the world, and in the last ten years, many Oriental vegetables have won places in Southern gardens. In some case, these vegetables are considered variations of food plants already well known, such as Japanese eggplant and edible green soybeans. But most Oriental vegetables are unique.

Working Oriental vegetables into your garden plan is as easy as working them into your menus. Most of them adapt best to intensive gardening practices — the same way they're usually grown in China and Japan. Grow them alongside or instead of your normal garden crops during every season of the year. In early spring, sow Chinese chives and snow peas. When the soil warms a bit, plant yard-long beans, Japanese melons, and hinn choy, or spinach amaranth. Later on, winter melons may be grown like pumpkins or winter squash, and transplants of Japanese eggplant may be set out. Chinese greens and radishes are naturals for the fall garden.

Grow and cook snow peas just like other garden peas, but give them higher support since they often grow more than six feet tall. Asparagus beans (sometimes called yard-longs) also need high stakes, so that the long pods hang freely in the air. The beans will grow up to four feet long if you let them, but they're best picked when about twenty inches in length and cooked like snap beans. Tender soybeans for eating green are another oriental treat. Blanche the green pods before shelling and they'll pop open much easier.

Many types of Chinese greens may be grown successfully in the South, but I suggest limiting these crops to the fall season. They bolt very quickly when grown in spring, and spring insects are tough on them, too. Chinese cabbage produces heavy yields when planted in early September. The loose heads stay in good condition through light frosts but burn when subjected to hard freezes. Bok choy (Chinese celery) is more cold-hardy and can stand temperatures as low as twenty degrees. Lei choy has thick, white ribs and tender green leaves. The different parts can be substituted easily for both celery and spinach in cooking. Sow these fall crops directly in the garden, for they do not transplant well.

Japanese melons and Japanese eggplants are particularly desirable, because the fruits are the perfect size for one person.

They are grown just like other melons and eggplants. Similarly, winter melons may be grown and eaten like winter squashes.

Turnip varieties from the Far East are so good that they're quickly replacing more Americanized strains in home gardens. *Tokyo Cross* and *Shogoin* turnips grow very fast, producing tender greens and mild, fine-textured roots. Daikon, or winter radishes, produce huge roots that are a staple in Japanese cuisine. Plant the seeds in early fall and harvest as you need them until the middle of winter.

Water chestnuts and bamboo shoots, two Oriental standards, require unusual cultural techniques and are not suitable for the average vegetable garden. Water chestnuts are a marsh plant, and bamboo is too cumbersome to fit into most gardens. However, both can be grown in the South if you provide an appropriate simulated environment. Check with suppliers of these unusual plants for suggestions on their culture.

Fresh bean sprouts never touch garden soil but certainly can be considered an Oriental vegetable. Whenever other Oriental vegetables are ready to harvest, start a jar of mung bean sprouts on your kitchen counter. Soak them overnight, drain, and then douse with water twice a day for three days. When the sprouts are the size you like, immerse them in a bowl of cold water and remove the seedcoats that float to the top. Rinse the sprouts and use them in stir-fried dishes and casseroles.

In addition to the vegetables I've mentioned, there are many other Oriental vegetables that have yet to be embraced by American growers. We can look forward to the introduction of many delicious vegetables from the Far East in future years.

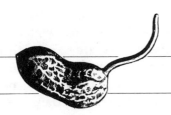

Peanuts

Peanuts are a fun crop to grow, if you have a wide swath of space available and don't mind a little weeding. They love our long, hot, growing season and produce very well when given proper care. Some people say you have to learn the "feel" of growing peanuts, the same way you learn to make bread — through experience. But if you understand these strange little plants and how they grow, there's every reason to believe that you will be successful on your first try.

Peanuts (or groundnuts or goober peas) originally came from South America, though they're now grown in every warm corner of the world. As hard-working legumes, they do a good job of foraging nutrients from the soil, and they generate most of the nitrogen they need. Still, they tend to grow slowly, especially during the first two months they're in the ground. It helps to kick-start the nitrogen fixing process by innoculating the seeds with bacterial innoculants (many seed companies pre-innoculate the seeds for you). Innoculation isn't necessary when peanuts are planted in a place where other legumes (beans and peas) recently were grown, because colonies of the right kinds of bacteria still will be in the soil. Since you don't plant peanuts until late spring, it's a good idea to plant them in place of expired English peas.

Peanuts do not need fertilization when they follow any crop that has been well fertilized. However, I do suggest adding some compost, greensand, or other mineral-rich fertilizer to the soil to ensure that trace nutrients are present. If you mulch your peanuts, water soluble nutrients in the mulch will trickle down to the roots, which also helps them to meet their dietary needs.

Peanuts demand warm soil for good germination and growth. Plant them during the month of May, at a time when your soil is dry and easy to work. Peanuts prefer sandy soil but do fine in clay, if it's not seriously compacted and contains organic matter. Loosen the soil thoroughly. (If it's clay, break up compacted places to a depth of sixteen inches.) Plant the whole, unscratched seeds one and a half inches deep, every eight inches. Plant in double rows if possible. Double rows (two parallel rows spaced one and a half feet apart but with wide spaces on the outside) are easier to weed and water than two widely spaced rows. They also look prettier.

One of the things peanuts need is regular weeding. They grow so slowly that it's easy for weeds to take over and choke them out. Start weeding early and weed regularly until the soil is thoroughly warm and the seedlings are strong. Work carefully when using a hoe, for the roots are close to the surface. You may decide to weed them by hand.

From this point on, the amount of work you must do to maintain your peanuts depends on whether or not you have a good mulch available. Hay is perfect, because it's easy to rake back and forth. The tricky part of mulching peanuts is that the mulch must be pulled back about a foot from the plants when flowering starts. The fertilized flowers turn into "pegs," which bury themselves in the soil and form peanuts. Obviously a thick mulch would get in their way. However, while the mulch is in place, it holds water in the soil, keeps out weeds, and prevents a crust from forming on the soil surface. If you pull back the mulch before the pegs form, the soil beneath the plants will be soft and crumbly — just the way the pegs like it. When all flowers have disappeared, you can push the mulch close to the plants again, being careful not to bruise any part of them.

Peanuts are pretty drought-resistant by nature, but there are two times when they crucially need water — just before flowering and just after the pegs enter the ground. In our climate, these events coincide with the drought season. Water your peanuts during these times, preferably with a soaker hose. Splashing water atop the ground increases the likelihood of soil crusting, and peanuts hate that. If crusting becomes a severe problem, lay down a mini-mulch of one-half inch sawdust around the plants.

Once the pegs have set, it takes about six weeks for

mature peanuts to form. Begin harvesting in late September or when the plants have been in the ground for one hundred thirty days, whichever comes first. Before you decide to harvest them all, dig up a plant at the end of the row and check the pods to see if they're ready. If so, get out your digging fork and get to work.

At harvest time, the idea is to pull up the entire plant intact. This is impossible to do when the soil is wet, so wait for a dry spell to dig your peanuts. Start by loosening the soil just outside the drip line of the plants. Then go back down the row and loosen the soil close to the plants. Pull them up one at a time and lay them upside-down in the sun so the roots will dry. Collect the peanuts you find loose in the soil, for these are ideal for boiling. Also pick small, slightly immature nuts from the plants and add these to the boiling pot.

Mature peanuts need to cure on the plants for two weeks or more. If the weather is dry, you can leave them in the garden, but it's safer to pile them in a place where afternoon thundershowers can't get to them. Pluck the nuts off when the pods become crisp, gently rinse them to remove some of the dirt, and spread them out on newspaper to dry for another week or so. Under very humid conditions, you may have to resort to using your oven to finish the curing process.

Peanuts are particularly good for your garden. Once the nuts have been harvested, the hulls and dead plants are excellent additions to the compost heap.

VARIETIES

Being early doesn't mean much with peanuts, for all peanuts take the entire summer to mature. Spanish peanuts are the fastest (one hundred ten days) but the yield is usually disappointing, since the nuts themselves are so small. The nuts of Valencias (*Tennessee Red*) are a little bigger, and some folks claim that the flavor of Valencias is superior to the other types. All things considered, Virginia-type peanuts are usually the most productive in our area, though they do tend to sprawl a bit as they grow. *Florigiant* and *Jumbo Virginia* are good varieties to try, especially if you're just getting started. Park Seed Company recently added a new variety to its collection called *Park's Whopper* which they claim is the biggest peanut yet.

Garden Peas

It's amazing to me how commercial canneries can turn delectable garden peas into tasteless mush, that bears only a slight physical resemblance to the real thing. Fresh picked peas are firm, flavorful, and very sweet. The most common complaint among gardeners is that they're so good to eat raw, very few of them make it to the table. The obvious solution is to plant more peas. They're one of the simplest vegetables to freeze, making it difficult (if not impossible) to grow too many peas.

There are three types of garden peas. First are English peas — the ones most of us visualize when we think of peas. Next in popularity among gardeners are Sugar Snaps, whose pods are as sweet and tender as the peas inside. Sugar Snaps are quite new; they were first offered for sale by major seed companies only a few years ago. I include them in my garden every year and recommend them to anyone who's slightly interested in growing peas. Snow peas, the original edible podded peas, are also an excellent touch in the home garden. All of these peas have similar cultural requirements. They mature at about the same time and may be planted twice a year — spring and fall.

Rule one with peas is to grow them only in cool weather. They will germinate at about forty degrees, which means you can plant them from early February to the end of March in our area. Peas can take a good bit of frost (unless they're in flower), and there is actually little danger in planting too early. If a late ice storm comes along and kills them, it's safe to replant seeds until about April 1. Most years you also can get a second crop of peas in the fall. During the last half of August, soak pea seeds overnight and plant them the next day. Keep the soil in the planting bed cool by mulching lightly with straw. Unless a hard freeze comes very early, fall peas can be harvested around the first of November.

Peas are legumes and therefore take an active part in feeding themselves by "fixing" nitrogen taken from the air in bacteria-powered "nitrogen factories" in their roots. This phenomenon has lulled some gardeners into believing two myths about peas: (1) Since peas are such great nitro-fixers, you don't need to fertilize them, and (2) Peas are such great nitro-fixers that they create enough nitrogen for themselves and for the crops which follow them. False on both counts.

The true story goes something like this: Peas sprout and begin to grow, and the roots use the nutrients present in the soil for this initial growth spurt. Gradually nitrogen-fixing bacteria already present in the soil (or present from the seed being innoculated with the same) colonize on the roots and begin the nitrogen-fixing process, storing excess nitrogen in nodules which form on the roots. When the plants begin to flower and reproduce, they start using this stored nitrogen, and they use most of it up by the time harvest is finished. So it is important to work some compost or manure into the soil at planting time; don't count on peas to feed crops that follow them.

Peas do not like highly acidic soil, and most Southern soils are pretty acidic. Apply lime to the planting site in fall or winter to raise the pH a bit, or work liberal amounts of wood ashes into the soil at planting time. Avoid planting peas near pine trees or other conifers — their yearly fallout creates very acidic conditions in surrounding soil.

Along with a sweet soil, peas require a good bit of air, both for the benefit of the nitrogen-fixing process and to prevent waterlogging. Oxygen in the soil is no problem if the soil is sandy, but in clay, it's important to cultivate well before planting and to scrupulously avoid compacting the soil by not walking on it while it's wet.

128

Peas use quite a bit of water, but they also can get too much. Following several consecutive days of rain in spring, you may notice some wilting leaves on your peas, particularly near the growing tips. This is a symptom of waterlogging. It should go away once the weather clears, especially if temperatures are still cool. If the weather stays damp for a long time, peas can mildew or fall prey to a number of fungi and diseases. These problems will not pop up if there is a reasonable amount of organic matter in the soil (to help drainage), and if the vines are staked to help air circulate, thus keeping the foliage dry.

VARIETIES

I recommend growing climbing pea varieties and staking every one of them. The bush-type varieties are all right, but their yield is small and they're difficult to pick (with the exception of *Novella* — more on that later). Vining peas produce more peas over a longer period of time — you'll get two good pickings (six days apart) from a stand of bush peas, whereas from a patch of runners the same size, you'll pick peas every other day, five or six times.

Rather than staking them, some folks allow short running varieties like *Wando, Laxton*, and *Green Arrow* to climb on each other. In many places, this is risky, for an upright mass of pea vines rarely makes it to maturity without being battered to the ground by strong winds. The only variety that's impressive without staking is the aforementioned *Novella*. It's a genetic oddball that produces very few leaves. Instead, it grows hundreds of tenacious tendrils which twist around one another. Blossoms appear on the outside of this ball of intertwined pea tendrils, so the peas are easy to pick.

The amount of staking required depends primarily on which variety is grown. *Sugar Snaps* are high climbers. The perfect support for them is five-foot chicken wire fastened between posts. *Giant Melting Sugar*, a good variety of snow peas to try, also needs tall staking or trellising, at least four feet high. Most English peas, however, grow only about three feet tall, so branches stuck into the ground at every third plant usually provide enough support. In spring, you also can use tomato cages as pea trellises. It usually works out that the tomatoes need the cages at about the same time the peas begin to expire.

A final argument in favor of trellised peas is that they're easier to pick. When picking, use two hands to keep from ripping down the vines. As with corn, the sugar in peas begins to turn to starch soon after picking. To get the very best peas, eat, cook, or blanch and freeze peas as soon as possible.

Field Peas

When days get hot and muggy and your early spring vegetables start to fail, it's time to plant field peas. Also called Southern peas, black-eyed peas, and crowder peas, they're the perfect vegetable to plant in hot weather, and no Southern garden should be without them.

Field peas are adept at resisting drought, since their main stems are slightly woody and retain water very well. Additionally, the leaves have a thick outer layer of cutin, so they don't lose too much water and wilt on hot days.

And if being drought-resistant isn't enough, field peas also meet their own need for nitrogen by "fixing" nitrogen from the air and storing it in their roots (they're legumes). If the soil is reasonably good to start with, field peas flourish with a modest addition of fertilizer. All you have to do for a good crop is plant, weed once or twice, and mulch with grass clippings or hay.

When you plant is important, for field peas will not grow in cool weather. Seeds planted in March or early April will sprout, but they won't grow vigorously until the nights warm up — usually late in May. Wait to plant field peas until most other garden crops are already in the ground. If you make one planting in May, a second one in early June, and a third one around the first of July, you should have a continuous harvest from late July until the beginning of October.

Even though they are almost self-sufficient when it comes to nitrogen, field peas do need other nutrients. Before planting, work some wood ashes and a little rock phosphate into the soil. Then plant the seeds one-half inch deep and four inches apart. In hot weather, it helps to soak the seeds overnight before planting and to plant them a little deeper than a half inch, especially in sandy soil that dries out fast.

Cultivate the soil around the seedlings when they're a few weeks old and thin them to twelve inches apart. Remove weeds and toss some of the loose soil from between the plants up around the young seedlings. As soon as the row is clean, mulch generously with grass clippings, hay, or something similar. If fresh grass clippings are used, keep them pulled back about four inches from the plants. However, mulch eighteen inches outward from the plants. Field peas sprawl a bit when fully grown, and any pods which touch the ground should rest on dry mulch, not on soil. That's all the work needed until it's time to pick the peas.

Occasionally you may feel compelled to water your peas, but the only times field peas really need water are just before flowering starts and just after the pods have set. When you water, soak the plants well. Shallow watering encourages the growth of roots near the surface, which in turn increases the plants' susceptibility to drought.

Very few pests bother field peas — partially because wasps hang around field peas, and most wasps are predatory. Sometimes Mexican bean beetles chew on the peas, but damage is usually light. The worst pests strike when the peas are ripe, boring holes into filled pods and laying eggs inside. You can beat these borers and other assorted pests by picking the peas as soon as they mature.

When picked slightly green, field peas have a buttery, creamy flavor; I think that's the best way to eat them. Extra batches may be blanched and frozen. Provided the weather stays dry and insects aren't bad, you can leave field peas on the plants until the pods become dry; then store and cook them as you would dry beans. However, in years when it rains a lot in August, mature peas may be ruined by molds and insects. Before this happens, pick and dry them in a warm oven until the pods are crisp. Put them in a paper bag, beat the bag with a shoe, and shell and sort the peas.

VARIETIES

All types of field peas do well in the South. Many of the newer varieties are disease resistant, and the trend is to breed strains which are low and bushy rather than vining in growth habit. Choose varieties according to the type of peas your family likes best, and keep experimenting until you find a favorite. *Pink Eye Purple Hull* is a good one to start with. The pods turn purple when they're ripe, so there's no guesswork at harvest time. *Mississippi Silver* and *Elite* are often described as cream types, for they are among the smoothest flavored of crowder peas. If flavor is your primary concern, by all means try *White Acre* or some other variety of "lady" pea. The peas are small, so there's more shelling to do, but it's worth the extra trouble. *California Blackeye* and *Magnolia Blackeye* are much more productive, since the peas are quite large, and they dry and store particularly well.

 # Peppers

Peppers are notorious for causing Gardener's Guilt — that feeling you get when your plants keel over from the weight of too many unpicked fruits. There are so many kinds of peppers (hot ones, mild ones, yellow, red, and green ones, juicy ones, thin ones, plus mutants galore, if you save your own seeds) that almost everyone likes at least one variety.

In the South, all peppers are easy to grow, provided you're patient with them. Neophyte gardeners worry when their peppers don't produce until late in the season, but that's just the way they are. Peppers are native to the tropics of Central and South America, where they grow as perennials. Perennial plants have the whole year to wait until the weather is just right for reproduction, and peppers grown as annuals do the same thing. Hybrid varieties in particular grow beautifully through the spring and summer, but they don't produce peppers until temperatures are just right — between sixty and eighty-five degrees. While the plants are ready to blossom by the middle of June, midsummer weather is usually so hot and dry that the blossoms drop off; or if they do happen to get fertilized, the peppers may be small and misshapen. However, once summer peaks out, all types of peppers produce fruit by the bucket. New varieties that do set fruit during very hot weather are being developed, and small cayennes and thin-walled types resist heat pretty well.

Bell peppers, banana peppers, and jalapeno peppers usually can be found in seedling form at garden supply stores. All other varieties must be started from seed. Peppers need warm temperatures to germinate, so start them indoors from early March onward. They also will germinate in a cold frame. Whether you buy your seedlings or grow your own, do not allow them to become rootbound. You can ease transplant shock of commercially-grown seedlings by planting them as soon as possible in large paper cups or other containers. All peppers should be hardened off for a week or so before planting.

Wait until the soil is warm before putting your peppers in the ground. In our warm climate, peppers do best in a clay type soil, which holds moisture for a long time. The most productive plants have extensive roots, often reaching two feet in all directions. Dig a big hole for each plant, so the roots can get off to a good start. Add one shovelful (but no more) of well rotted compost or manure to each planting hole and take a few minutes to work it in well. After the plants recover from their move and start growing, mulch them with hay or straw.

Peppers have very few serious insect enemies. Many insects sample pepper leaves, but they don't like them too well and quickly move on to other crops. But unrotted organic matter, be it mulch or green compost, can cause problems for peppers. A terrible fungal disease called *southern blight* lives comfortably in partially decomposed organic matter, and it's murder on peppers. The symptoms are wilting of the plants for a few days, followed by sudden death. If you then pull up the affected plant, you'll see that the base seems to have been eaten away by a whitish dry rot. Often the disease spreads to a few neighboring plants and then stops. The best controls are to make sure that organic fertilizers used on peppers are completely rotted, and to keep mulches pulled at least two inches away from the plant base. You also should not rotate peppers with lima beans.

Since they grow all summer before they really start producing, pepper plants are quite large by the time they bear fruit. The weight of the peppers often causes the plants to fall over. While it's fine to stake them up, you may get better yields by letting the plants fall over onto a thick mulch. The sunlight available to the leaves increases when the plants are lying down. As long as the peppers and leaves don't touch bare soil (where they will rot) and there's plenty of leaf cover to protect ripening fruit from sunburn, the peppers will not suffer from a reclining position.

Besides letting them sprawl a bit, you can stimulate production by harvesting the green ones as soon as they reach pickable size. Most peppers turn red if left on the plant. The red color emerges as the chlorophyll breaks down. Although red peppers contain a little more vitamin C than green ones, they tax the plant's resources for as long as they stay on the plant. Pick the earliest peppers green and wait until the season winds down before allowing fruit to ripen to full color. Most varieties need forty-five days or more to grow a mature pepper from a fertilized flower. After Labor Day, you can pinch off blossoms that won't have time to mature before frost, which will leave more plant energy going to those that will.

Pull up all pepper plants just before the first frost and let the remaining peppers ripen on the dead plants. Peppers turn red even faster on the uprooted plants, and they start the drying process when hung in a warm, airy place.

Peppers may be eaten fresh, dried, frozen, or pickled; the best method of preservation depends on whether the pepper in question has thin or thick walls. Thick-walled peppers, like bell peppers and pimentos, freeze especially well, though they also may be dried. Hot peppers usually have thinner walls, which means they dry fast and keep well. However, handling them can be dangerous. The hot substance (capsaicin) causes severe physical pain, especially if it comes in contact with mucous membranes, eyes, or other tender places. It won't wash away with soap and water, though some folks say scrubbing pepper-burned hands with milk helps. Always wear rubber gloves when handling the hot ones, and try to deal with super-hots without cutting them open — the interior seeds and pulp are much hotter than the skin. Instead, make a slit in the side of thin-walled cayennes and chilies to allow air to circulate to the inside and dry them whole.

What about saving your seeds? Pepper seeds taken from fully ripened, red-colored peppers are usually dependable sprouters. However, seeds taken from hybrid plants probably will not grow into the same kind of peppers you think they will, especially if you grew several other kinds of peppers at the same time the hybrids were grown. Peppers cross-pollinate very freely, and parentage of homegrown seeds can be very difficult to determine. However, this means that you can develop a custom strain for yourself. Plant two non-hybrid varieties whose characteristics you would like to see shared side by side, away from your other peppers. Save some of the seeds and plant them the next year. Many people do this with hot peppers to develop a strain with just the right amount of heat to suit their individual taste.

VARIETIES

It would be difficult to name a pepper variety that does not do well in the South. However, disease resistance can be important, and most people grow resistant hybrids, especially when it comes to bell peppers. A partial listing of these includes

Keystone Resistant Giant, Yolo Wonder L, Bell Boy, and *Emerald Giant*.

Other mild peppers such as *Sweet Banana, Cubanelle, Dutch Treat, Gypsy*, and Italian peppers or pepperoncini are a very desirable addition to the pepper patch. They are extremely productive, so don't get carried away and plant too many.

Hot peppers grow even better than sweet ones, and it's unlikely that your family will use more than will be produced by two plants. You can assume that the smaller and hotter the peppers are, the more the plants will produce. Try *Cayennes, Tabasco* peppers, *Jalapenos*, all chili types such as *Anaheim*, and any other variety that strikes your fancy.

Potatoes

Potatoes often are maligned as being fattening, and by the time you drizzle butter and sour cream over them, or make a bowl of potato salad laced with mayonaisse, they are. A plain potato, however, is actually 99.9 percent fat free and contains numerous vitamins and minerals. Potatoes that have been in storage for a while may need dressing up to make them taste good, but not so with freshly-dug potatoes. They're full of natural flavor and need very little to transform them into a taste treat.

Many folks also think you need a big garden to grow potatoes, but that's true only if you plan to grow several bushels. In fact, by using intensive cultivation methods, it's possible to grow several pounds of potatoes per square foot. So you'll need only a little space to give your family the pure pleasure of eating fresh potatoes.

Potatoes grow best during the cool, wet days of spring. Most people wait for a break between spring rains and plant their main crops in March, but sometimes the weather won't cooperate, and it's impossible to get them planted. To avoid this, I recommend pre-planting in late fall. If winter weather kills a few, it's easy to poke replacement potatoes into the row in spring. If a freaky winter kills all of your fall-planted potatoes, the row can be replanted in spring without being recultivated.

There are almost as many ways to grow potatoes as there are types of potatoes. However, in our damp climate, one planting method increases yields and produces good, sound potatoes better than any other method — growing them in excavated trenches filled with mulch.

To do this, work up the row and dig out a trench about five inches deep and twelve inches wide. Rake about an inch of rotted manure into the bottom of the trench. Then lay the potatoes in the trench and cover with at least a foot of straw, leaves, or other mulch material. When planting in spring, cut seed potatoes into pieces and plant these. When pre-planting in fall, however, plant only whole sprouting potatoes. As long as you see no evidence of diseases, it's fine to use sprouting potatoes leftover from midsummer diggings. It's best *not* to use whole potatoes for spring planting. The problem is that the parent potato turns into a blob of gray mush just as the new potatoes reach maturity, which takes a lot of the fun out of poking around under the plants with your fingers.

Newcomers to potato culture sometimes are alarmed when their potatoes get knee high and then fall over, but this is natural. In fact, if your potatoes don't fall over, you may have a problem — probably too little sunshine. The best time to add extra mulch is just before and just after the plants bend down. Potatoes swell in the area where the main stem turns to roots, and this part of the plant should be protected from sunshine at all times, even if it means dumping an armload of grass clippings into the middle of the plant.

Of course, you don't *have* to grow potatoes in trenches and cover them with a mulch. Many gardeners prefer to grow potatoes in plain soil and hill-up the soil around them as they grow. This works fine, but it requires more work and tends to limit the size of the potatoes. When planted in trenches, potatoes need little or no watering and weeding. As the tubers develop, they swell within the soft environment of the mulch rather than in heavy soil. Regardless of the planting method used, it's usually necessary to add mulch or additional soil when the plants are almost mature to keep sunlight from reaching the potatoes, which push toward the surface as they grow. Sunlight causes potato skins to turn green, and green potatoes contain a toxin that can be harmful to humans and animals.

Potatoes are fully ripe when the foliage begins to die back and the skins on the tubers are thick enough to be called skins. But you don't have to wait until this happens to start enjoying your crop. Carefully "rob" the parent plants of small potatoes anytime after blossoms appear by feeling around near the base of the plants until you find a good-sized potato. If you're gentle, the plant will go on growing, sending strength and energy to the smaller tubers you leave behind.

Don't worry if your potatoes don't blossom. Making seed is a standby reproductive ploy that potatoes use when they're feeling fiesty, and some varieties are simply fiestier than others. Potatoes reproduce so effectively with their roots that flowering just isn't necessary most of the time. There should be no significant difference in the size of the harvest between plants that have flowered and those that have not. The only problem with non-flowering potatoes is that you have to guess more when deciding if they're ready. Gently pull back the mulch or soil whenever you feel like it and examine what's going on down under.

Besides discovering little potatoes, you probably also will discover one of several potato-eating insects at about the time the plants blossom or fall over, whichever comes first. The most common ones are (1) Colorado potato beetle larvae, (2) blister beetles, and (3) harlequin bugs. Small, black, flea beetles also may appear, but they don't do much damage. The Colorado potato beetle larvae, commonly called potato bugs, may be hand picked. See page 22 for control measures for this pest. Blister beetles and harlequin bugs may be run off by timely applications of rotenone, and they're also big enough to hand-pick pretty effectively. Blister beetles have a substance in them which causes skin irritations in some people, so don't squash them in your bare hands no matter how mad you get. I collect mine in an old juice can with a half inch of gasoline in it; they don't last long in there. But handpicking is not for everyone, so if you can't stand touching bugs, stick with rotenone. Any "hard" pesticides you use are going to get on your potatoes and will wreak havoc with the earthworms and other critters that keep the soil soft for the ultimate benefit of your potatoes.

Start digging the potatoes as soon as they reach good size. If you have too many, dig out every other plant and heap extra mulch around those that will stay in the ground for awhile. If the tops are suffering from heavy insect attack and the potatoes beneath them are ripe, cut off the tops and mulch over the potatoes. This will keep them safe until you have a chance to pick them up. Don't try to scrub freshly dug potatoes, because the skins will roll right off. Cure them first by bringing them into a dark, air-conditioned place and letting them air-dry for two weeks or longer to toughen the skins. Scrub the potatoes just before you cook them, or take them all outside and wash them with a forceful spray from the hose. Potatoes can still "green up" after they're cured, so be sure to dry them in deep shade and store them in a place that's cool, dark, and dry.

VARIETIES

In garden supply stores, seed potatoes usually are described as either red or white. Most of the time the reds will be *Red Pontiac* and the whites will be *Kennebec*, both of which are well suited to the South. Seed catalogs offer a broader choice, including the *Explorer* potato, which is grown from seed each spring, much like a tomato. Many Southerners don't trust white potatoes and grow only red ones, since the reds are earlier and more reliable than whites in our climate. I grow both types because their flavor and textures are different. Red potatoes are best for boiling and frying, while whites are unsurpassed as bakers and for mashed potatoes.

Idaho potatoes, usually *Russet Burbanks*, will grow in the

South if given special care. Plant them in a very soft soil that contains a good bit of leaf mold.

Pumpkins

Only a few hundred years ago, pumpkin-like fruits were a staple item in regional native diets. In fact, American Indians cultivated pumpkins — North America's contribution to the cucurbit clan — along with winter squash, which are like pumpkins in many respects. Nowadays few people even know what hot, buttered pumpkin tastes like (it's delicious), but most of us are familiar with *real* pumpkin pie. It doesn't take long to get addicted.

Growing pumpkins is kid's stuff. They come up dependably, grow steadily for a long time, and almost always produce a nice collection of fat, orange pumpkins. Most people like to grow the big ones, though the smaller varieties are usually better for eating. Regardless of size, pumpkins are among the simplest cucurbits to grow, since they naturally resist the belligerent attacks of cucurbit-loving insects.

Pumpkins contain huge amounts of vitamin A and other nutrients, so you should grow some for eating as well as for cutting into jack o'lanterns at Halloween. They need plenty of space. You can allow the vines to run into the grass at the edge of the garden, or you can plant them among widely-spaced corn. Plant in hills at least six feet apart, and enrich the hills with compost or manure and a little ground rock phosphate, if you have it. The giant pumpkins which win ribbons at county fairs have been given the benefit of copious amounts of fertilizer, without which they would reach only average size.

Plant pumpkins in warm spring soil at about the same time you plant beans. They require one hundred or more days to reach maturity, which means that those planted in early May will be ready at the end of August. If you want them to mature later, wait until the first of June to plant them. Keep weeds away from the seedlings until they begin to sprawl and can claim their own space.

Squash bugs may bother pumpkins, especially the new bush or short-runner types which resemble squash more than traditional pumpkins. Field pumpkins are relatively unattractive to this pest, and are a safer bet if you intend to plant your pumpkins and then neglect them.

Pumpkins are ripe when their rinds cannot be easily punctured with a fingernail. The vines also begin to wither as the fruits become mature, and the stem attached to each fruit becomes dry. Cut the ripe pumpkins from the stem with a knife, leaving two inches of the stem attached. As it dries, it will form a barrier to bacteria and molds and thus help to prevent rotting. While most pumpkins will keep for several weeks at room temperature, humidity can cause problems in long-term storage. To be on the safe side, cook and freeze extra pumpkin meat while you're certain the pumpkins are still sound.

VARIETIES

Most field pumpkins — the seeds of which may be proudly presented to you by a farmer friend, whose deep roots in the land have caused him to name his strain "Tennessee Field Pumpkin" or "Georgia Field Pumpkin" or "Alabama Field Pumpkin," etc. — are well worth growing. Seeds of any open pollinated plant that's been cultivated locally are a safe bet, but decide what you want to do with your pumpkins before choosing a variety. Field pumpkins are a good choice since you can eat them, carve faces in them, and save the seeds for snacking. However, if the seeds are what you're after, plant *Godiva, Trick or Treat*, or *Triple Treat*, which have hull-less seeds. Some of the best pie-making varieties include *Sugar Pie* and *Small Sugar*.

Radishes

The only problem with growing radishes is that it's easy to plant too many. Radishes mature fast and all at once, and they stay in peak condition for only a few days. You probably can produce enough radishes by interplanting them with other vegetables. In early spring, seed them into carrot and spinach beds. Later, place a few in or near cucurbit hills, for radishes reputedly repel cucumber beetles. In our climate, you can plant radishes continuously from mid-February until early April, and again in fall during the month of September.

The best radishes grow fast, without having to endure the stresses caused by low soil fertility, shortage of water, or unsuitably hot or cold temperatures. Although they are not particularly heavy feeders, you'll get better quality radishes by working a little rotted manure into the bed. Organic matter also helps the soil to hold onto water, and radishes need a constant supply of water.

Radishes are enthusiastic germinators and usually need to be thinned so that they stand two inches apart. If left to grow on top of each other, they develop little if any root and go to seed ahead of schedule.

Harvest your radishes as soon as the roots swell. If left in the ground too long, they become woody, hot flavored, and they split. Those grown in cool weather are crisper and milder than warm-weather radishes.

VARIETIES
Plant fast-maturing varieties such as *Cherry Belle* and *Scarlet Globe* both spring and fall. Winter radishes (they're more pungent than salad radishes) do best as a fall crop only, for they taste best when they mature in cool weather. Winter radishes also keep in the ground much better than the fast-maturing

142

types. Varieties to try include *China Rose, Black Spanish*, and *White Chinese*.

 ## Rutabagas

Rutabagas are tricky to grow in the South, so you won't see them in many home gardens. However, it can be done. Rutabagas take three months to mature, and during their last month of growth, the weather needs to be cool. It's therefore best to plant them for fall harvest.

The biggest problem in growing rutabagas is getting the seeds up. They must be planted in late summer (July and August), and the seeds have understandable difficulty germinating in hot, dry weather. For best results, soak them overnight before planting, and cover the bed with damp burlap bags or newspapers for a few days after planting the seeds one-quarter inch deep.

Rutabagas do best in sandy soil that is not extremely acidic. Plant them in any location where drainage is excellent, and use only fully rotted organic materials to enrich the planting site. Unrotted organic matter may cause the roots to rot when they're almost ready for harvest.

The plants grow quite large and should be thinned to stand at least eighteen inches apart. Mulch lightly with grass clippings or small leaves to help retain soil moisture. The roots may be harvested as soon as they reach softball size — usually about ninety days after planting. Sound, mature rutabaga roots will keep under refrigeration for several months.

The only rutabaga variety that's widely available is *American Purple Top*. Although they don't taste exactly like rutabagas,

143

turnips and yellow beets are simpler and faster to grow and make a good rutabaga substitute. Interplant them among your rutabagas and decide firsthand which you like best.

 # Salsify

Few Southern gardeners are familiar with this unusual vegetable. It's sometimes called *oyster plant*, for the cooked roots have the subtle flavor of oysters. Salsify is an excellent addition to the garden, since it can be dug in winter and spring when other fresh vegetables are scarce. The only way to find out if you like it is to grow it yourself, for salsify is almost never sold in grocery stores.

The seeds also may be difficult to find. Many of the large mail order companies sell them, but they probably will not turn up on the seed shelves of you local garden supply store. Plant the seeds in late summer, and give them the same treatment as carrots. The roots mature in about three months. When cold winter weather comes, mulch over the bed but allow the tops of the plants to poke through the mulch.

Dig your salsify roots carefully during the winter and early spring months, when the soil is dry. At full maturity, the roots are one inch in diameter and about eight inches long. They look like hairy white carrots. Refrigerate them if you don't plan to cook them for several days, and peel them before steaming or boiling. Add salsify to soups, casseroles, and other dishes, or eat them steamed and lightly buttered.

144

Spinach

As Popeye taught millions of children in his cartoons, spinach is a super-nutritious vegetable. And in Southern gardens, spinach has another virtue unparalleled by any other food plant: It can be picked in prime condition three or more months of the year. All you have to do to get this kind of production is to plant at the right times.

Spinach is basically a winter vegetable. It needs cool weather and short days to develop good flavor and texture. If you like spinach, you'll want to plant it three times each year — early fall, mid-fall, and again first thing in spring. Fall plantings made in late August are ready to pick in October and November, and the plants will winter over and produce again in early spring. Plantings made in early October will not produce pickable leaves before cold weather stops their growth, but the seedlings will stand through the winter and produce a very large crop in March. You also can plant spinach in late February for spring harvest, but plantings made after the first of March will bolt before you have a chance to gather many leaves.

Plant your spinach in an enriched, well-drained bed. Dig in rotted manure or compost prior to planting, especially for fall-planted spinach that will stay in the ground for a long time. Sow the seeds thickly and poke them in about one-half inch deep. Germination time depends on the weather and the variety grown, but generally you should expect to see some seedlings within ten days. Water the bed from time to time if rain is scarce, and pull out weeds by hand if there are too many. When the plants have two true leaves, thin to five inches apart and mulch to keep out weeds.

Start picking your spinach, one leaf at a time, when the plants have more than five good leaves. At full maturity, you can pick up to half of the leaves on each plant at a time. New leaves emerge rapidly from the plants' centers, and heavy rains or supplemental watering help accelerate their growth.

Fall-planted spinach easily withstands temperatures as low as ten degrees. Many leaves get burned by hard freezes, but the plants survive in spite of this damage. However, the plants do not really grow when the weather is very cold, so unless you're growing it in a cold frame or unheated greenhouse, don't count on picking spinach in the middle of winter. The first spring picking from plants that have wintered over will be remarkably sweet and crisp.

The spinach harvest ends when the plants bolt and produce flowers. They do this in April, just as days become long and warm. Watch for early signs of bolting and gather your remaining spinach as soon as you see any changes. When the bolting process begins, the new leaves that emerge from the plants' centers will be smaller than usual. Then the main stem will begin to elongate, and within days a tight, green eye will become visible in the center of each plant. If left alone, the stem will grow upward and produce flowers. Spinach leaves lose their crispness as soon as bolting begins, and as the reproductive cycle gets into full swing, they become bitter, too. When that happens, pull them up and chop them into the compost heap.

VARIETIES

Southerners need fast growing varieties of spinach, since our cool weather seasons are so short. *Dixie Market*, (available from Hastings) is the fastest-maturing spinach I know of, and it also winters over well. *America* and *Melody* are excellent hybrids that are so vigorous they will produce up to six heavy pickings. The *Bloomsdale* strains are much too slow to grow well in the South.

New Zealand Spinach is not at all like regulation spinach. It grows in warm weather and does not tolerate frost. However, it does taste like spinach when cooked, which is really the only way to eat it. (When growing spinach primarily for eating raw, stick with real spinach.) Plant New Zealand Spinach in mid-spring or early fall. It reseeds itself readily and is a good "unweed" to naturalize in the garden. New Zealand Spinach is

146

also an excellent, edible, green manure crop for summer, since it always produces many more leaves than you're likely to pick.

Squash

There seems to be no middle ground on squash — people either love it or they hate it. But few Southern gardeners, even if they're not personally fond of squash, pass up the opportunity to grow a little.

SUMMER SQUASH

Summer squashes come on fast, produce a heavy yield in less than eight weeks, and then die. During the two-to-four-week period when it's producing, a single zucchini plant may produce ten pounds of food. That's a pretty good return from one little seed. Many gardeners grossly underestimate the productive capacity of squash plants and grow twice as much as they need. It's an easy mistake to make.

Summer squashes will grow in almost any type of soil but prefer a sandy, well drained location. One shovelful of manure or compost per plant is sufficient fertilizer for these short-lived vegetables. The seeds may be planted in hills or rows and should be thinned as they grow, so that the leaves barely touch. If possible, thin when the plants have three true leaves, for afterwards they grow very fast.

Watch the plants closely for the first squash bugs and cucumber beetles. As soon as they appear, begin dusting periodically with wood ashes, and pick off any bugs you see. Dust or spray with rotenone if needed. See squash borers on page 27 for ways to control this pest.

When the plants begin producing, harvest squashes at least every other day. The prickly leaves cause some people to itch. If this is a problem, pick only when the foliage is very dry and wear a long-sleeved shirt. The more you pick, the more strength the plants will have to grow more squash. Extra squash may be frozen, dried, or pickled. Squash blossoms are edible, too, and make lovely garnishes.

Don't waste your time and energy trying to save squash plants that are over the hill; plant some more instead. Since they mature so fast, summer squash may be succession planted from springtime until the middle of August. However, a bare hint of frost will kill them.

VARIETIES

When most people think of squash, they think of either yellow squash or zucchini. Dramatic variations of these old favorites are now available, including *Gold Rush* (a yellow zucchini), and *Gourmet Globe*, a delicious, sweet, round, summer squash of zucchini ancestry that tastes ever so slightly like a melon.

No matter which summer squash variety you choose, harvest the fruits when they're slightly immature, before the seeds and rinds harden. *Yellow Crookneck* or *Early Prolific Straightneck* should be picked before the rinds turn a bright orange color. *Dixie* is an extra-early yellow squash that always performs well. Among the green zucchinis, *Aristocrat* and *Seneca* are impressive varieties. Don't forget to keep them picked! *Scalopini* is a new squash that has a richer flavor than other scallop types. *Early White Bush* and *Peter Pan* hybrids are good varieties of the patty pan type.

WINTER SQUASH

Winter squashes grow in the heat of summer, just like summer squashes. However, the mature fruits are quite different — more like small pumpkins. They're closely related to pumpkins and share the nutritive value, keeping quality, and savory flavor of pumpkins. Most are native plants of North America, though plant breeders have improved them immeasurably in recent years.

Any squashes that eventually develop a hard, impermeable rind with dense inner flesh are categorized as a winter squash, since they will stay in good condition long past the time when autumn turns to winter. Winter squashes contain less water and more fiber than summer squashes, which also improves their storage ability.

Winter squashes grow similar to either pumpkins or summer squash, depending on whether the variety grown has long, vining runners or a short, bush-like growing habit. Nowadays, it's stylish for winter squashes to be bushy, and new varieties are introduced every year which exhibit this feature. Bush-type winter squashes are great for saving space, but they tend to be a little more susceptible to insect attack than the vining types.

It takes four to eight weeks for a winter squash to reach full maturity, once the flower has been fertilized and the fruit has set. Consequently, winter squashes need more fertilizer than comparatively short-lived summer squashes. Add plenty of compost to the planting area, along with a little ground rock phosphate and wood ashes. These mineral additives help the plants to take up other nutrients that are present in the soil, which in turn helps guarantee that the fruits will be firm and sound with a good rind.

Winter squashes may be planted in late spring along with other cucurbits, or you can wait until July to plant them for fall harvest. Be sure to leave adequate space between hills for the plants to run. When planting in spring, when rain is plentiful, germination should be no problem; but later in the summer, when the sun goes full blast from sunup to sundown, heat stress on germinating seeds becomes severe. The problem may be partially solved by planting the squashes in partial shade. Soak the seeds overnight before planting, and water the hills every day until the seedlings emerge. If a summer drought is in progress when the plants are young, water them every other day until they begin to run.

Squash bugs sometimes attack the succulent young seedlings of winter squash. Timely dustings of wood ashes and handpicking may be necessary to keep them at bay. Later, when the plants are older and the stems are tougher, these insects will have a harder time sucking the life out of them. You'll still need to watch for them and possibly spray or dust with rotenone to bring them under control.

Generally speaking, the longer it takes winter squashes to mature, the better they will keep after harvest. The extra maturation time usually results in a very thick rind. However, many winter squashes may be picked when immature and used much like summer squashes, though their flavor is different. *Butternuts, Hubbards*, and a few acorn types make interesting side dishes when eaten when very young. A new variety, *Jersey Golden Acorn*, tastes a little like corn when eaten within days after the pretty yellow fruits have set.

Midsummer plantings sometimes benefit from being pinched back, which enables the plants to send energy to ripening fruits, rather than setting new blossoms that won't have time to mature before frost. Remove new blossoms which appear after mid-September to encourage maturation of half-ripe squashes.

If winter squashes are to be stored, leave them on the vine until they're fully mature. They are ripe when the stems turn brown and the rind is so tough that you can't scratch through it with your fingernail. Cut the squash from the vine with a sharp knife, and leave an inch or so of the dried stem attached to each fruit. Carefully clean them by wiping with a damp cloth, and allow them to dry in a cool, airy place. After a couple of weeks, wipe each one with a cloth that's been lightly sprinkled with vegetable oil to further protect the rind from molds and bacteria. Winter squashes, harvested in August from spring plantings, should be handled the same way. Store them indoors where it's cool.

VARIETIES

Choose winter squash varieties according to your personal taste. The different types vary in how long it takes them to mature, with acorns requiring only seventy to eighty days, compared with more than one hundred ten days for Hubbards.

Butternuts fall somewhere in the middle, usually requiring around ninety days to reach full ripeness.

Along with these traditional winter squashes, you also can grow spaghetti squash — it's inner fibers easily shred into pasta-like strings after cooking, and they have a mild, un-squashy flavor. *Kuta*, a new specialty variety, is similar to a spaghetti squash when fully mature, but in the meantime can be used as a summer or winter squash. There is also a remarkable new squash variety called *Sweet Mama*, which is neither acorn nor butternut nor Hubbard. It's prolific, sweet, and different, with a space-saving bush growth habit.

Sunflowers

These tall, dramatic flowers are more than just a pretty touch in the vegetable garden. Most varieties produce large, edible seeds. In addition to their value as food plants, sun-flowers also can be used to help other garden crops. Plant them a few weeks ahead of runner beans, and use them as bean stakes. Or plant sunflowers on the south side of melons or other crops as a sunscreen. Many people plant them around the garden's edge, where they make attractive border plants that also function as a windbreak.

Sunflowers are very easy to grow, though you'll have to put forth extra effort to produce huge specimens worthy of the county fair. Plant the whole, uncracked seeds one inch deep in April or May. If you add compost or rotted manure to the planting site, the plants will be taller and the flowers larger. After the plants are up, thin them to stand at least twelve inches apart, and mulch them with hay or grass clippings to help hold water around the roots and reduce competition from weeds.

Most of the large-flowered varieties produce only one, giant flower per plant. Leave the flower on the stalk after the petals fall since the seeds continue to ripen for several weeks afterwards. The first sign of ripeness comes when the backs of the flowers change from green to pale yellow. At this point the seeds around the edge of the flower begin to dry and loosen, and birds may start pecking them out. Cut the ripe head from the stalk, leaving about a foot of stalk attached. Then hang them in a dry, airy place to finish ripening. Check the heads every few days, especially if the weather is humid. The pithy backs of the flowers absorb moisture and sometimes cause the seeds to rot. Place the heads in full sun on hot dry days to speed up the drying process.

When black stripes show clearly on the seedhulls, it's time to remove the seeds. Rub and twist the dried flowers to remove them. Then dry the seeds in a warm oven for a half hour before storing them in jars. If some flowers show signs of mold and mildew, return these seeds to the garden instead of saving them for eating. Throw them randomly in the garden, and a few will make it through the winter and show up as volunteers in the spring.

VARIETIES

Mammoth and *Giganteus* are the best known varieties of giant sunflowers. They often grow more than ten feet tall and are perfect to use as bean stakes. *Sunbird* and *Sunburst* don't grow as tall, but they produce large flowers with big, plump seeds. These shorter varieties are especially useful as sunscreens. There are many other types sunflowers, but they're designed to produce pretty flowers rather than edible seeds.

 # Sweet Potatoes

Southern summer weather is the enemy of many garden vegetables, but not sweet potatoes. They thrive in hot, humid weather. And the same acidic clay soil which has to be modified before you can use it for many vegetables is just the kind of home that sweet potatoes prefer. This wonderful plant manages to take the worst of summer and use it to advantage. It's no wonder that in early August, sweet potatoes are the prettiest, healthiest, and most promising vegetable in the garden.

Today's disease-resistant sweet potatoes are the result of decades of research. Characteristics of various ancestral strains from tropical corners of the world have been selected and refined to the point where growing a good crop is child's play. The only part that's labor-intensive is getting them started, but even that is an interesting little project if you understand what you're doing.

Unlike white potatoes, sweet potatoes do not grow from sprouting eyes. Instead, leafy shoots emerge from the parent potatoes, and eventually roots grow from the places along the shoots where leaves meets main stem. To propagate them, start by laying whole parent potatoes in a nursery bed. The bed can be a place in the garden that's been excavated a few inches deep and filled with sand, sawdust, or chopped leaves, or you can use a box, or even a pile of chopped leaves. What's important is that the potatoes stay warm and moist, and that shoots have a soft medium in which to grow. Start the nursery bed in March, since it takes several weeks for good shoots to develop.

The first shoots should appear about a month after the potatoes are set out in a nursery bed. When they're about six inches long, cut them from the parent potato. Also remove the bottom inch from each slip, even if it has roots growing on it. This particular section of the slip sometimes harbors disease organisms, so dispose of it in the compost heap. Immediately plant the slips in shallow trenches, laying them in sideways so that only the top two leaves show above the soil. Even if you get them planted just before a rain, the slips probably will look like they're dead a few days after you plant them. Most of the time they're fine, and within two weeks healthy plants should grow from each slip. Meantime, a second cutting of slips should develop in your nursery bed. If you buy your slips, keep the roots damp at all times. Also remember to cut off the bottom inch of each slip before planting. Sweet potato slips may be set out until the middle of June.

Sweet potatoes do not require rich soil. In fact, too much nitrogen can reduce the yield of big tubers. However, sweet potatoes do need large amounts of phosphorous and potash. These are easily supplied by working rock phosphate and wood ashes into the planting site. Once the plants are established, mulch heavily with hay or grass clippings. A good mulch usually will eliminate the need for both weeding and watering, and it also helps to keep the soil soft and conducive to the development of chunky roots.

After the plants have been in the ground for two months or so, some root sections will begin to change into potatoes. As the potatoes reach full size and hot weather ends, the above-ground vines stop growing and turn yellow. This usually does not happen until the end of September. Yellowing leaves late in the season is a sure sign that tuber development is in full swing. The longer you leave them in the ground, the larger the tubers will grow. Dig your sweet potatoes about the time of the first fall frost. Potatoes often are found a foot or more from the plant base, so start your digging from the outside of the row. Be very careful not to bruise or prick the potatoes, and don't leave them lying in the sunshine, either. Move them to a warm, dry place, and allow them to cure for two weeks. Then store them indoors where the temperature is at least fifty-five degrees.

VARIETIES

The most widely grown varieties are *Centennial* and *Jewel.* The sweet potato slips that you buy at the local garden supply store are probably *Centennials.* Like *Jewel,* these potatoes have orange flesh and copper skin. *Jasper* and *Goldrush* are also dependable varieties which resist rot. If you prefer yellow fleshed sweet potatoes, plant *Porto Rico.* It does not resist disease as well as the others but is usually very productive. These are the most common varieties, but there are many others with unique characteristics that can be grown successfully in Southern gardens.

Swiss Chard

Swiss chard is a beet relative, although it does not produce an edible root. The rest of the plant, however, is infinitely edible. Raw or cooked, the main leaf stems make a decent celery substitute. Chard leaves are quite beautiful and can be used in place of spinach, or cooked Southern-style with onions and salt pork. The thing that distinguishes chard from other cooking greens is that it doesn't lose its flavor in warm weather. When the spring spinach is long gone and fall turnip greens are months away, the chard is perfect for picking.

Chard is not a heavy feeder and will do well even if the soil is slightly infertile. The seeds are large and have no trouble germinating under adverse conditions. Plant them in spring and again in early August. As with other greens, a few feet of row or a bed three feet square will easily supply all the chard your family is likely to eat.

Young plants look like a cross between spinach and Chinese cabbage. Weed the bed or row a few weeks after planting so you'll know how many seeds came up. If there are bare spaces, drop in a few more seeds. Begin picking outer leaves when the plants are as big as a small stalk of celery. Swiss chard can take many small pickings, for new leaves grow from the centers of the plants very quickly. You also can cut it all at once, and then new leaves will appear within a week, just like turnips or beets.

Very few insects or other pests bother Swiss chard. When the plants start to deteriorate, chop the whole plant off at the root nub. If you have too many, chard greens and stems may be frozen.

VARIETIES

For such a simple vegetable, chard varieties have fancy names. *Lucullus, Fordhook,* and *Swiss Chard of Geneva* are the most common ones. Rhubarb chard (it has red stalks) is so attractive that it may be planted in flowerbeds.

Tomatoes

Tomatoes are the No. 1 vegetable in gardens nationwide, primarily because they grow so well in backyard gardens. And, of course, because they're delicious. Here in the South, it's one of the few vegetables that you can plant in spring and pick from until frost. But I think songwriter Bobby Bare said it best: "Two things money can't buy are love and home-grown tomatoes."

Over the years, various methods of growing tomatoes have come in and out of gardening vogue. For a while, it was traditional to let them sprawl, and statistics support the belief that free-growing tomato vines produce more fruit per plant.

But sprawling tomatoes tended to get out of hand, and soon people discovered that pruning and staking resulted in cleaner, easier to manage crops. Nowadays, most Southern growers agree that a combination of these two methods is the easiest way to grow tomatoes in our climate. By either caging tomatoes or propping them on a fence, the vines grow as freely as they would if allowed to sprawl, but they also get stake-like support from the cages. This method consistently works best for me.

Before getting into specifics about how to grow tomatoes in cages, there is another angle that deserves some discussion. In the South, it's important to grow more than one variety of tomato in any given year. Tomatoes are sensitive to a number of environmental factors, the most important of which are temperature and rainfall. In our climate, there is no way to predict whether the summer will be wet or dry, hot or mild, or a combination of all. Every tomato acts differently in different types of weather, so by growing several types, you reduce the risk of having an overall poor crop. For example, the *Better Boy* variety (the most popular hybrid tomato) does fine as long as summer rains don't come in sudden deluges. However, if your whole tomato patch is *Better Boy,* and all you get is heavy rain, you'll see a lot of blossom-end rot and cracking. Had you included a few *Red Cherries* or *Romas,* (which adjust to wet conditions), you at least would have had *some* good tomatoes.

Another trick to getting a full, long harvest of tomatoes in our region is to stagger planting dates. Most people still plant their tomatoes all at once, which results in a bounteous yield that tends to end a little prematurely. The advantage to saving some space for later plantings is that you are assured of a good fall harvest. There are years when tomatoes grow so well early in the summer that they wear themselves out by midseason. From that point onward, they produce only a few small fruits. By having younger plants in the ground, which are just beginning to bear when the older ones are on the wane, you are assured of tomatoes for as long as warm weather holds out. Late plantings also insure that you'll have plenty of mature green tomatoes to ripen indoors and enjoy through the first half of winter.

A common question is whether it's better to grow determinate or indeterminate varieties. Determinate is to tomatoes what bush beans are to beans; that is, they mature early, grow to a certain size, produce, and then die. Indeterminate is to tomatoes what runner beans are to beans; that is, they take longer to mature but then produce over a long period of time. Since our growing season is so long, it's best to grow predominantly indeterminate varieties, though determinates are good for freezer crops and for fall planting, since they mature fast and all at once.

Tomatoes are easy to start from seeds, and that's the only way to include special varieties in your garden. Tomato seedlings are surprisingly easy to handle, and once you get the hang of it, my guess is that you'll never buy seedlings again.

Tomatoes are quite tropical and cannot tolerate frost at all, so there's no point in starting too early. In February and March, plant seeds indoors in any kind of container that has drainage holes in the bottom and won't dry out easily. I start mine in small styrofoam cups and then transplant them to larger cups before moving them to the cold frame for hardening off. Tomato seedlings are very susceptible to damping off, so be careful not to over-water them, and see that they are adequately ventilated. Seedlings are big enough to move to the garden when they have about six true leaves.

If you do buy seedlings, choose specimens that show no signs of blossoming. Very small plants simply aren't big enough to support the energy drain involved in reproduction, and they will sit in the ground wondering what to do while you puzzle over why they aren't growing. Sooner or later they will grow, of course, but the maturation process will be delayed, since the plants essentially "start over" in their growth cycle once they're planted.

Another consideration when planting tomatoes is the temperature of the soil. Tomatoes demand warmish soil and may fall victim to fungal diseases if set out too early. Generally, the time to place the first transplants is April, and then they usually need to be protected from wind. You can provide this protection *and* give tomato seedlings the illusion of summertime by placing cloches over them. Gallon-sized plastic milk jugs with the bottoms cut out are perfect for this, since warm, damp air that accumulates in them can escape through the open cap of the jugs. If you use another type of cloche, be sure to allow for ventilation.

Transplanting tomatoes correctly is probably the biggest favor you can do for your crop. If the soil in your garden is red clay, it pays to improve the drainage by digging in sand, rotted sawdust, or extra compost. Tomatoes sometimes have trouble taking up the calcium they need in tight clay soil — a problem that's aggravated if the soil is very acidic. The result of this condition is large black splotches on the blossom end of the fruits. Play it safe by digging several shovelfuls of compost into each planting hole, and add a handful of wood ashes if you did not lime the space the previous fall.

Tomatoes grown in sandy soil need extra compost in their planting holes, too. Since sandy soil drains so well, water soluble nutrients leach out quickly. Tomatoes stay in the ground for a long time, so it's important to provide three or more shovelfuls of rotted manure or compost for each plant. Dig a hole at least one foot square (the bigger the better), and work in whatever organic fertilizer you decide to use.

After the planting holes are prepared, place the seedlings as deep as possible so that only a small topknot of leaves sticks out above the soil line. Roots grow from the buried part of the stem, which helps give the plants a head start at developing a large root system. The more roots grow below the soil, the better chance you have of getting large, high-yielding tomato plants.

Tomatoes should begin to grow vigorously a week or so after transplanting. This is the time to mulch them and to set up cages or a fence. I use six-foot lengths of six-inch mesh-welded wire, bent into cylinders about two and a half feet in diameter, as cages. The large mesh is easy to reach through to gather tomatoes and insects, and it's also easy to clean at the end of the season. Fences do a good job of supporting the sprawling vines, though the vines often need to be tied to the fence — a step that's not necessary if you use cages. Either method is superior to staking, since less pruning and other maintenance is needed. If tomatoes are planted right and given good support, the only care they require during the season is mulching, picking, and possibly pruning in midseason.

A good mulch is more beneficial to tomatoes than to any other garden crop, because tomatoes are super-sensitive to changes in the amount of water in the soil. Mulches help to regulate the flow of water in the soil by retaining water when the weather is dry, and by soaking up excess water in wet weather. Without a mulch, the water content in the soil varies so much that tomatoes develop problems with blossom-end rot, blossom drop, cracking, and several soil-borne diseases. If you don't mulch anything else in the garden, see that your tomatoes are securely tucked in with a thick blanket of mulch.

After tomatoes have been planted, caged, and mulched, all you have to do is to wait for the harvest to begin. Tomatoes usually produce a large number of fruits, once they get going. But right around harvest time, insects can become a problem. The critters that I have the most trouble with are blister beetles — black bugs with yellowish stripes that eat tomato leaves until their stomachs bulge. When there aren't too many of them, handpicking works well, especially if the plants are grown in cages. Shake the cages a little, and most of the blister beetles will drop to the ground, where they're easy to collect and drown in gasoline. Sometimes blister beetles appear in very large numbers, however, and they will even munch on beans if they run out of tomatoes to eat. Rotenone gets rid of most of them, though I use it only when necessary.

The tomato hornworm is another pest which occasionally devastates tomatoes in our region. These are large, colorful caterpillars that eat tomato leaves. They also host a beneficial wasp larvae, so if you see only a few of them, it's best to leave them alone. However, if hornworms are devouring your bushes, one application of Bacillus thuringiensis (see cabbageworms) will give them a terminal bellyache.

Tomatoes planted in April usually produce a large harvest around the first of July. Once this main crop is gathered, it's time to renew the plants and get them ready to produce a fall harvest. To do this, cut out old, leggy stems and failing limbs, ultimately reducing the size of each plant by about one-third.

Then let the plants rest for a few weeks. In early August, give them a feeding of manure tea or fish emulsion fertilizer. If you skip this midsummer pruning, your tomatoes probably will continue to produce anyway, but the tomatoes will be small and of inferior quality. When the plants channel their energy to only a few healthy limbs, they tend to produce bigger and better fruits and also are less susceptible to insects and diseases. One suggestion, though: Wear old clothes when pruning tomato plants, for they bleed a green juice that stains anything it comes into contact with.

Some folks don't like to mess with this pruning; instead, they pull up plants after they've finished bearing their main crop. New tomato plants for late harvest can be set out to replace old ones as late as the Fourth of July, but it's best to get them in a little earlier. Give these late tomato plantings the same care and maintenance that you provide for spring plantings — mulch, cage, and pick as they ripen.

Sometimes fall comes early and frosts threaten the plants before most of the tomatoes have had a chance to mature. If the plants are in cages, plastic sheeting draped over them can keep the plants from being damaged by light frosts. A hard freeze, however, spells death to tomatoes, so gather every tomato left on the vines *before* the first killing frost. Then sort through them and set aside those that are perfect and appear to be almost ripe. As long as the skins of these mature green tomatoes have not been broken by insects or weather, they gradually will ripen and turn red. The flavor of tomatoes that are ripened indoors is not as good as vine-ripened specimens, unless they're one of the new varieties (like *Long-Keeper)* that have been developed especially for this purpose. When setting out late tomatoes that you plan to harvest while still green, by all means, try one of these special varieties.

VARIETIES

Choosing varieties can be very confusing, since there are more than a hundred tomato varieties to choose from. I suggest experimenting with as many types as you can. Though I try to stick with varieties that are disease resistant, I'll try any variety once. Here are the results of some of my experiences.

161

HYBRID TOMATOES

The super-hybrids that are resistant to everything (denoted by VFN and TMV next to the name, meaning resistant to verticillium wilt, fusarium wilt, nematodes, and tobacco mosaic virus) are usually quite dependable, although a little boring. For slicing tomatoes that need to look as good as they taste, I suggest *Better Boy, Earli Girl,* and *Terrific.* Beefsteak types that have built-in disease resistance are now available and are great for slicing. Beefsteaks are unusual in that their flowers are double, which means that the tomatoes themselves are sort of like Siamese twins — two tomatoes merged into one. Because of this, they sometimes grow into funny shapes, but they taste fine.

Besides slicing tomatoes, I grow salad or cherry tomatoes and paste tomatoes. In the salad category, my favorite is *Red Cherry* (a non-hybrid). It's sweet but still tastes like a tomato. Some of the new salad hybrids are so sweet that they taste like a fruit, which is fine if that's what you're after. Once in a while, you may run across a salad variety that tastes very acidic. These are the seed packets to throw into the garbage can.

The latest thing in little tomatoes are varieties developed for growing in pots and baskets. Patio tomatoes are stocky, determinate plants that won't run like regular tomatoes; therefore, they can be placed in large pots or in flowerbeds without creating a lot of clutter. The varieties for basket culture produce cherry-sized tomatoes, usually in clusters. Failure with basket grown tomatoes is usually caused by too little light — they need plenty of sun. Of the patio types, the first ones (introduced a few years ago) were short in the taste category and really never have caught up. But just as with garden tomatoes, keep trying them all until you find a variety that tastes the way you want it to.

When considering these little tomatoes, remember that they have been bred to grow in a semi-protected environment and may fail if grown in an open garden. Around the patio, however, these tomatoes can be tasty and beautiful. If the plants look fine but they're not setting fruit, it may help to hand pollinate the blossoms. On a warm, dry day, gently "paint" the insides of all open flowers with a small, dry paintbrush.

Paste tomatoes, sometimes called Italian tomatoes, are small, pear-shaped tomatoes that have very few seeds and a lot of pulp. They are very easy to grow and are perfect for canning and making sauces. Both *Romas* and *San Marzanos* are disease resistant, and I plant some of both every year since *Romas* do great when the weather is dry and *San Marzanos* produce better in wet weather than any tomato I've tried. If you've been canning slicing tomatoes, you'll be delighted at the thick sauce that you can get from these varieties of paste tomatoes.

STANDARD TOMATOES

Our grandmothers and grandfathers had no disease-resistant hybrid tomatoes in their garden. The varieties they grew were all standards, and each summer they collected a few of the best tomatoes in the garden and saved their seeds for next year's crop. Every spring, volunteer tomato plants popped up here and there in the garden, and Grandma likely as not let these volunteers grow to maturity. We still can do this today. Some people believe that standard varieties have better tomato flavor than hybrids, and in many cases, that's true. However, the biggest advantage of standard tomatoes is that the seeds can be saved from year to year. Or better yet, the garden can save the seeds for you.

Standard varieties also present the opportunity to develop a strain that is particularly suited to your garden — one with the exact flavor, size, and growing habit that you prefer, and one that grows well in your garden's special environment. All you do is select the tomatoes that you like most and save them. To extract viable seeds, squeeze the inside of a tomato into a glass and stir in half again as much water. Let this sit overnight. The next day, carefully remove all the gunk and seeds that have floated to the top, then dry the seeds you find at the bottom on paper towels. Shuffle the seeds around as they dry to keep them from sticking to the paper. Store them in a cool, dry place, and there you have next year's tomato seeds. But that's the hard way to save tomato seeds.

The easy way is to bury your selected tomatoes in the fall wherever you want them to grow the following spring. For this to work well, first prepare a tomato planting hole the same way you would in late spring. Then plant the whole tomato about two inches deep, and mash it if you like. The tomato itself will rot, but several seeds should make it through winter and germinate at the perfect time in spring. This procedure saves time that you otherwise would spend starting seedlings and transplanting them. There is no better argument than this for growing standard tomatoes.

The case against standard tomatoes is that they are not as disease resistant as most hybrids, and that they tend to stop producing altogether in midseason. Fortunately, plant geneticists have not forgotten standards in their quest for the perfect tomato, and several standard varieties have been introduced recently that match the best hybrids in terms of disease resistance. The problem with longevity can be solved partially by giving the plants a good pruning in midsummer. As long as you give them a rest, standard tomatoes will come back from a rather comatose period in July and August and produce good tomatoes until frost.

Turnips

When most folks think of fall gardening, the first vegetable that comes to mind is turnips. In fact, turnips have become the flagship vegetable in most fall gardens. All you have to do is plant and water them, and they grow like magic.

Plant your main crop of turnips in late August or early September in any type of fertile soil. Scatter the seeds over a wide bed, rather than planting them in single rows. The seeds should be barely covered with soil — it's usually sufficient to drag a rake over the seeded bed. When planted in a matrix like this, the leaves shade the surrounding soil as they grow, which helps to keep out weeds and protects plump young roots from the sun.

Turnips grow very fast and tender young greens are ready to pick about a month after planting. Regular rainfall helps to speed them along. Cool weather improves the flavor of both greens and roots, so you may want to wait until nighttime temperatures drop into the forties to begin harvesting turnip greens.

Begin gathering a few of the outer leaves from each plant when the leaves are four inches long. If you don't care for turnip roots, it's fine to gather as much as two-thirds of the topgrowth at a time, but pick lightly if you want to grow large, tender roots. If a sudden frost damages the leaves too badly, remove all of them and water the bed thoroughly; you should have a vigorous second crop within a few weeks.

Turnip roots develop within two months after planting. The best-flavored bulbs are those that grow fast in cool weather. Harvest the roots when they are two inches in diameter or larger, and gather all of them before hard freezes begin. Turnips like cool weather, but they cannot handle temperatures below twenty-five degrees. Roots left in the ground too long lose their fine texture, and they're often attacked by soil insects.

Turnips also may be planted in the spring, but the results will not be as impressive as when they're grown in fall. Many spring insects feed on turnips, chewing ragged holes in the leaves. Also, the roots of turnips planted in spring are usually small and not as sweet as those grown in fall. It's best to plant only leaf-type turnips in spring, and to plant them as early as possible.

VARIETIES

Choosing the right variety is the key to a successful turnip crop. Several varieties have been developed which produce only greens. These include *Seven Top* and *Crawford.* They produce greens so vigorously that they can be cut down completely with a lawn mower, after which they will grow a second crop of tender, young leaves.

Most people like both greens and roots, and there are several outstanding dual-purpose varieties. *Tokyo Cross, Just Right,* and *Purpletop White Globe* are excellent choices. The greens are tender and flavorful, and the roots are crisp and mild. A new hybrid, *Shiro,* boasts extra-sweet roots that are perfect for eating raw.

6
WHERE TO GET WHAT YOU NEED

As with other endeavors, the best gardening resources usually are other people — friends, extension agents, or the man down the street who fed his family of six from his garden during the Depression. But beyond the sharing that takes place among gardening friends and neighbors, there are many people in the horticultural industry who are ready to provide you with merchandise and expertise that can help to make your garden better.

The first place to shop for materials is your local garden supply store. Mineral fertilizers and soil additives are bulky, so it's easiest to buy them close to home. I also like to see how gardening tools feel before buying them — something you can do only in a store. Take the time to get to know the people and products at local lawn and garden centers.

You also may be able to buy locally-grown vegetable seedlings. The South is dotted with hundreds of small nurseries, many of which grow vegetable seedlings in season. Most of these are small family businesses, so you may have to ask around to find them.

There are several reasons to buy seeds and plants through mail-order seed companies. The biggest advantage is the wide selection of varieties available. Looking through a few seed catalogs is the best way to find obscure herbs, heirloom vegetable varieties, imported vegetables, and state-of-the-art hybrids. Here are a few of my favorite seed companies and their specialties:

SOURCES FOR MAIL ORDER SEEDS
H.G. Hastings
P.O. Box 4274
Atlanta, Georgia 30302

167

This company's "Seedsman to the South" logo is no joke. They specialize in the best varieties for the South, including old favorites and the newest hybrids. Hastings' spring catalog is a "must" for every serious Southern gardener, and they also publish a smaller catalog in the fall. Hastings warrants the quality of all of their seeds, and their commitment to Southern growers is unquestionable. Their modestly priced *Vegetable Growing Guide* provides a wealth of information on growing vegetables in the South.

Park Seed Co., Inc.
Greenwood, South Carolina 29647

The Park family markets a huge selection of disease-resistant, highly productive varieties of vegetables, flowers, and fruits. They specialize in "High Performance" varieties that grow well in the South, including many exclusive varieties available only through them. Their scrupulous business practices and fast, dependable delivery make them a joy to work with. Most of Park's small seeds come in patented Parkspaks® — foil envelopes lined with plastic that make seed storage foolproof.

W. Atlee Burpee Co.
300 Park Ave.
Warminster, Pennsylvania 18974

This large national company has been in business since 1876. Over the years, Burpee has never missed a chance to market innovative varieties, and they deserve credit for many advances in plant breeding that we now take for granted. Burpee carries almost any vegetable you may want to grow, and all of their seeds are guaranteed.

Vermont Bean Seed Co.
Garden Lane
Bomoseen, Vermont 05732

With a name like Vermont Bean, you expect the biggest selection of beans around . . . and you get it. Offerings also include numerous varieties of corn and peas that you won't find elsewhere. Delivery is incredibly fast. This company sponsors a Garden Clinic Service, too. You pay for the call, but you're able to reach a skilled garden consultant by just picking up your phone.

Nichols Garden Nursery
1190 N. Pacific Highway
Albany, Oregon 97321

Nichols specializes in herbs and rare seeds. Their herb listings are extensive, including six different varieties of mint. This is also the place to look for oriental vegetables and unusual gourds. In addition to vegetable and flower seeds, Nichols sells supplies for making cheese, beer, wine, and potpourri.

Thompson and Morgan
P.O. Box 100
Farmingdale, New Jersey 07727

Although this company has a Northern orientation, they do offer suggestions to Southern growers for their somewhat unusual varieties. Thompson and Morgan sells many European varieties, as well as new hybrids, most of which are near the top of their class when it comes to flavor.

Johnny's Selected Seeds
Albion, Maine 04910

Johnny's primary goal is to meet the needs of Northern growers. Many of their vegetable varieties may not be perfect for the South, but this company also markets garden-sized bags (four pounds) of several grains and clovers — perfect for mini-plantings, cover crops, or green manures. Johnny's sells several heirloom vegetable varieties that the larger companies have dropped from their listings.

SOURCES FOR GARDENING INFORMATION

The more you garden, the more gardening questions you'll have that demand answers. Seed companies usually provide basic information on how to grow certain vegetables, and you also can find a few gardening reference books at your local library. Additionally, gardening expertise is there for the asking at your local county Extension Service office. Extension Service literature is usually free and can be picked up at the county office or ordered by mail. Organic growers sometimes are offended by the chemical orientation of Extension Service recommendations, but bear in mind that such information is of considerable value to commercial growers.

Besides Extension Service publications, there are several magazines, books, and organizations of special interest to vegetable growers. Following are some of the best magazines:

Organic Gardening
33 E. Minor Street
Emmaus, PA 18049
In my view, this is one of the top gardening magazines published today. Monthly coverage includes the latest research findings and many firsthand reports from adventuresome, backyard growers.

Horticulture
300 Massachusetts Ave.
Boston, MA 02115
This beautiful magazine will appeal to anyone passionately interested in plants. It includes in-depth articles on various plant species and methods for cultivating them.

Flower and Garden
4251 Pennsylvania Ave.
Kansas City, MO 64111
This magazine is changing with the times, with more pages now dedicated to coverage of vegetables and annual flowers. It's still quite inexpensive, too.

REFERENCE BOOKS

Magazines are fun, but oftentimes what you need is a good, sound reference book. I highly recommend *Organic Plant Protection* from Rodale Books of Emmaus, Pennsylvania, 18049. Other excellent Rodale selections include *Seed Starters Handbook* by Nancy Bubel and *Rodale's Color Handbook of Garden Insects* by Anna Carr.

Garden Way Publishing of Charlotte, Vermont, 05445, publishes a huge series of booklets on everything from growing

170

onions to making compost, as well as numerous larger volumes. Garden Way also markets tools, carts, tillers, and other gardening supplies.

ORGANIZATIONS

Gardens for All
180 Flynn Ave.
Burlington, Vermont 05401
    The goal of this national non-profit organization is to promote home gardening. Members receive a monthly newsletter, which includes articles on every imaginable aspect of growing your own food as well as other seasonal tips to help solve gardening problems. Gardens for All members also have the opportunity to buy gardening aids and books at slightly discounted prices.

Regenerative Agriculture Association
222 Main Street
Emmaus, Pennsylvania 18049
    This non-profit organization's objective is to take organic gardening a step further by helping farmers and small growers develop ways to incorporate safe, low-cost, organic methods into their operations. Membership includes *New Farm* magazine, published seven times a year.

INDEX

ABOUT THE AUTHOR

As Southern Correspondent for *Organic Gardening*, one of the nation's leading gardening magazines, Barbara Pleasant writes the monthly calendar column for the South and Gulf regions. She also is a regular contributor of articles on a wide range of gardening subjects; meanwhile, she continually conducts trials and experiments in her half-acre garden.

Barbara Pleasant was born and raised in Mobile, Alabama, and now lives and gardens near Huntsville, Alabama.